This introduction to Greek tragedy, the origin of much of our modern drama, is the work of a remarkable scholar who is also a practical man of the theater. Maurice Valency is the author of magisterial studies of Ibsen, Strindberg, Chekhov and Shaw, and of a magnum opus, *The End of the World*, an account of the astonishing career of symbolism in the theater, from the nineteenth century to our times. He has written for the stage and for television, and he translated, adapted and collaborated in producing two great Broadway successes— Giraudoux's *The Madwoman of Chaillot* and Dürrenmatt's *The Visit*.

On the subject of tragedy there is in fact some need for a candid guide. Here is a passage from the opening pages of the book that describes the nature of the problem that confronts the reader who seeks enlightenment:

"...In our day the Greek tragedies are chiefly read in translation, and translation, it goes without saying, is at best a dubious transaction. In the case of the most brilliant versions, the creative talents of the translator are normally in evidence to the point where we may safely assume that what is offered in a modern tongue is virtually a modern poem. Of the various translations available in English, each bears the distinguishing mark of its time and author. The best are truly admirable works of art. None succeeds in conveying the tone, or even the sense, of the original Greek.

(Continued on back flap)

TRAGEDY

TRAGEDY

Maurice Valency

NEW AMSTERDAM

New York

Published in the United States of America by
New Amsterdam Books
171 Madison Avenue
New York, NY 10016

Printed in the United States of America.

First printing.

10 9 8 7 6 5 4 3 2 1

This book is printed on acid-free paper.

Library of Congress Cataloging-in-Publication Data

Valency, Maurice Jacques, 1903–
    Tragedy / Maurice Valency.
        p. cm.
    ISBN 1-56131-009-3 (alk. paper)
    1. Greek drama (Tragedy)—History and criticism.   2. Theater—
Greece—History.   3. Aristotle.   Poetics.   4. Tragedy.   I. Title.
PA3131.V35   1991
882'.0109—dc20   90-40014
                                                        CIP

CONTENTS

PREFACE

THIS IS A book about tragedy for those who know little about it. For those who know much about it, there exists, of course, an extensive and richly effervescent body of critical writing with which I have no wish to meddle. In this book I have concerned the reader only with what are—or should be—the elementary aspects of the subject.

One ventures into this field with some trepidation. Tragedy is properly within the domain of the Hellenists. Nothing serious can be said about it without some recourse to the Greek. But this view of the matter necessarily excludes a considerable proportion of those who are interested in tragedy not as a branch of philology or archeology, but primarily as drama. If in venturing to explore the subject from this standpoint I must trespass on territory that is already quite adequately charted, my excuse is that, while there is no lack of learned literature in the area, there does appear to be some need for a primer. A primer, that is to say, for adults.

In putting these chapters together I had it in mind to clarify some of the doubts that have occurred to me in the course of my reading. In this sort of work one is not always brilliantly successful. The result is sometimes a position more exposed and more uncomfortable than the system of sturdy sterotypes in which one customarily takes refuge in doubtful circumstances. To doubt, in the words of Montaigne, is as good as to know. But it is not at all the same thing.

In quoting from the plays and the *Poetics* I have relied mainly on the text of the *Loeb Classics,* which is readily accessible, I believe, everywhere. With respect to the *Poetics,* however, I have had frequent recourse to the texts established by Gudeman and by Rostagni. The interpretations of Butcher, Bywater, Cooper, Fyfe and Gilbert have been of immense assistance in the elucidation of doubtful passages. I have not hesitated to make use of the English translations of the tragedies wherever I found the text perplexing, and I am especially indebted in this regard to the brilliant work of Lattimore, Arrowsmith, and Grene. To these poets and scholars, and to those others of whose talents I have silently availed myself in organizing these pages, I express my heartfelt thanks.

New York   M.J.V.
1990

TRAGEDY

TRAGEDY
AND THE TRAGIC

TRAGEDY IS NOT a term that rewards definition. In a general way everyone knows what it is. Specifically it is indefinable. Comedy is meant to be understood. It speaks, more or less intelligibly, to the intellect, and save in its lowest forms, it provokes discussion. Tragedy, however, is directed to a deeper and more primitive mental level than the faculty that endeavors to make sense of things. Like music, tragedy does not, at its best, make statements. It arouses sensibility. It is not meant to be understood. It is meant to be felt.

In comedy the line that divides the pathetic from the ridiculous is seldom sharp, so that it is possible to cross the emotional frontier from tears to laughter without official sanction. In the case of the great comedic masterpieces the reader is invited to share an Olympian viewpoint from which the pathos of the comic and the absurdity of the pathetic are equally apparent. But while laughter and tears are readily accommodated in comedy, tragedy is less amenable. It deals, of course, with the absurd, but not from the airy heights of the intellect. It is a chthonic poetry, a poetry that searches the depths of our experience, its darkness.

Tragedy is rooted in ancient Greece. Specifically it is associated with the Attic theatre of the fifth century B.C. Nothing comparable developed, it would seem, in any other time or place. It is true that cultures that have come under Buddhist influence have in some way approximated the Greek idea of tragedy as we know it. But the magic of the Nō plays, their mood and mystery, are fundamentally alien to our Western way of thought, and this magic barely reaches us. What is essential in Greek tragedy, however, touches us closely. The darkness through which Oedipus groped his way to Colonus is a darkness we know. With respect to his sadness, not much has changed in the course of the centuries. It may be that we do not entirely understand his tragedy. It is nevertheless our own.

Unhappily, what we know of Greek tragedy rests so heavily on scholarly reconstruction that we cannot easily dismiss the suspicion that our idea of the ancient drama is a relatively modern conception. We have no way of assessing with confidence the Greek idea of the tragic or the extent to which the surviving texts represent it. The handful of plays that have survived the centuries is a meager remnant of what was once a rich and widely varied literature. The texts that were transmitted were edited and reedited by generations of schoolmasters in Alexandria and Byzantium and ultimately established by Western scholars, each of whom necessarily set his stamp on the stuff he handled. Virtually insurmountable barriers, linguistic and cultural, separate us from those who savored this poetry twenty-five centuries ago, and the widely disparate interpretations with which the most competent classicists sometimes render the same text testify to the nature of the consensus. It is under these conditions that we study a body of dramatic poetry that in power and beauty has never been surpassed.

Moreover, in our day the Greek tragedies are chiefly read in translation, and translation, it goes without saying, is at best a dubious transaction. In the case of the most brilliant versions, the creative talents of the translator are normally in evidence to the point where we may safely assume that what is offered in a modern tongue is virtually a modern poem. Of the various translations available in English, each bears the distinguishing mark of its time and its author. The best are truly admirable works of art. None succeeds in conveying the tone, or even the sense, perhaps, of the original Greek.

If, in translation, Greek tragedy nevertheless makes a convincing impression, it must be because, in spite of everything, it is impossible to suppress the universality of its conception. Every age arranges the world in accordance with its lights; but essentially the furniture of the universe remains the same. The stuff out of which the Greek poets made tragedy has changed, certainly, in the course of the years. The tragic myths do not speak to us with the authority they had in the days of their currency, but as symbols of what goes on in the human soul they serve their turn as well as ever. Their sound, it is true, is now no more than a whisper. But there is no need for them to shout.

An abyss of time, seemingly unbridgeable, separates us from those who wrote in the time of Sophocles, but there is nothing to be gained by seeking to modernize their utterance. The theater has lost something, doubtless, since it was sacred to Dionysus, but it has not lost its magic. The vein of tragedy pulses powerfully across the centuries. The distance, of course, is there. Though the agony of Oedipus and the fury of Medea can be kindled in our theater as vividly as ever, as characters Oedipus and Medea are no longer quite within reach. Possibly they never were.

The terms *tragic* and *tragedy* are inextricably entangled. They are not synonymous. Tragedy is a dramatic genre. The tragic is a poetic mood. Greek tragedy was a musical play based on a dramatic poem in high style, designed for production by a company of actors and a chorus of dancers. The form, apparently indigenous to Attica, was already developed in the sixth century B.C. It flowered brilliantly in the course of the next century and died away during the years of the Macedonian empire. Of the handful of Greek tragedies that have survived, all are in high style. All deal with a serious subject. But not all are tragic. Some have a happy outcome. Some might properly be called melodrama. From a thematic viewpoint tragedy evidently had a wide spectrum.

Its pattern was rigid. Greek tragedy was not designed as a public entertainment. It was a sacred rite. In Athens, in the time of Aeschylus, nine tragedies were selected annually for production in a dramatic contest in honor of the god Dionysus. The plays, subsidized by the community, were presented in a sacred precinct under religious auspices. In these circumstances the dramatic form necessarily resisted innovation. From its first examples in the fifth century to the last plays of that era the form of tragedy was invariable.

Since tragedy consisted of a series of scenes which developed a plot, it might well be considered a narrative genre. Its matrix, however, was lyrical. The dramatic action unfolded through the interplay of the acted scenes and the songs and dances of the chorus, accompanied by the flute and the lyre. The effect must have been predominantly musical, operatic.

The lyrical basis of tragedy is usually ascribed to its origin in the dithyramb. Dithyrambs were musical compositions sung on festal occasions by a choir of men grouped around the altar of Dionysus. Supposedly the ode became dramatic at some time in the course of its development when it occurred to the leader of the chorus, the exarch, to designate one of the singers to engage him in dialogue. As an explanation of the origin of tragedy this leaves something to the imagination, but it has the merit of accounting for the peculiar form of the tragic genre—

an alternation of acted episodes in verse and lyrical passages sung by a choral group.

A tragedy normally began with a prologue, a brief recital designed to orient the audience with regard to the story that was to be represented. The prologue was usually spoken in iambic verse by a single actor who addressed himself directly to the audience, but sometimes it took a more elaborate form involving spectacle and dialogue, virtually an introductory scene of the play. At its close, the chorus filed into the orchestra, the dancing-place, singing its opening song, the parodos. It occupied the orchestra throughout the performance.

The parodos was followed by the entrance of the actors, and the play began. The acted episodes were spoken usually in iambic trimeter, a meter that approximated the rhythms of oratorical speech. Greek actors did not speak in prose. At the end of their scene the actors withdrew, and the chorus sang a stasimon, a standing-song, consisting of a series of stanzas, in complex rhythms, which normally had some connection with the plot.

At the end of this ode, the actors appeared, and played an episode, after which the chorus again took over. There were usually five or six episodes, interspersed with as many odes, but there was apparently no rule as to the permissible number of scenes. There were no act divisions. The play proceeded without interruption over a period of perhaps two hours. When it came to an end, the actors withdrew, the chorus sang a closing song, the exodos, and left the orchestra. Presumably there was applause.

The formal structure of tragedy is evidenced by all the surviving plays and is easily reconstructed. The tragic effect which this drama was designed to produce, however, is elusive. In the *Poetics* Aristotle writes of the tragic effect in terms of fear and pity, but it is difficult to describe in such terms our emotional response to the *Oedipus* plays or the *Medea*.

In Greek tragedy the tragic effect is usually the result of a shattering experience, but the tragic in tragedy is by no means a pathos that belongs exclusively to the theater. On the contrary, it echoes the melancholy that pervades classic literature from the time of Homer. It is the sadness that pervades Western poetry from its earliest expression to the sentimental romanticism of the present day. As the Greek chorus has it: "Best of all it is not to have been born, and next best to have died young." The mood is familiar, a commonplace that, among other things, blurs the distinction between what is acceptably tragic in tragedy and what is rejected as merely pathetic or sentimental.

The distinction is emphatic, but even at best, it is never entirely clear. The tragic is, of course, a subjective experience, but it has a collective aspect and is necessarily subject to social influences. In classic tragedy we are invited to share the pain of kings, and in this identification we are in some sense exalted—a flattering experience. A bourgeois setting precludes this effect. In comparison with the agony of Oedipus, the sorrows of Rosmer are apt to seem trivial. In the *Poetics* Aristotle limits the tragic protagonist to the class of those "who enjoy great reputation and prosperity." In our day such people are apt to be bankers and merchants. Human nature, doubtless, has not changed essentially since the time of Aristotle, but social conditions have altered to the point where it has become possible to portray tragically those who were once considered the subject of comedy. But in tragedy played on this level the feeling of grandeur is lost. What remains is a sense of the sadness of existence, a deep and poignant pathos, but not the tragic of Greek tragedy.

Not much has been preserved of the ancient poetry, and what remains is such that it is impossible to characterize its tone with authority. The tragic mood is ambiguous. It is both abject and aggressive, both submissive and defiant. Other artistic genres celebrate the joy of life. Tragedy deals in sorrow. It conveys the feeling that life holds no promise of security or stability but that, in spite of all, it befits a man to live with dignity and to die with decency. These are, of course, outward displays and necessarily theatrical. But behind the tragic mask is a reality which cannot be hidden, and cannot be voiced, but only suggested. It is significant that it was long ago considered important to make of this a display in sacred surroundings for the contemplation of a god.

GREEK TRAGEDY

I N THE TIME of Petrarch, Greek was virtually unknown in the
Western world. Nobody knew how to write a play. Italian
scholars were eager to read Homer, whom Dante had hailed as
Virgil's master, but few scholars had heard of Aeschylus.
Learned men from Byzantium came rarely to Italy, and those
who came seldom lingered. In 1396, however, Manuel
Chrysoloras came to Rome on a clerical mission and was induced to give a course in Greek at the Studio in Florence. He
proved to be an inspiring teacher, and students from all quar-
ters of Italy came to Florence to study with him. This marked
the beginning of the Greek renaissance in the West. The rest
went quickly.

By 1429 Cardinal Bessarion had established a base for Byz-
antine scholarship in his palace in Rome. Twenty years later we
find Demetrius Chalcondylas lecturing on Plato in Perugia,
while in various Italian cities Greek studies were being carried
on with vigor. By this time there was an avid demand for Greek
books in Italy, and astute scholars and book dealers were jour-
neying back and forth between Venice and Byzantium bringing
bales and chests full of Greek manuscripts home for sale.

In 1423 Giovanni Aurispa, at this time a diligent young

student, brought back to Italy a battered manuscript of seven plays by Aeschylus. This codex, copied about the year 1000, eventually found its way to the Laurentian library in Florence. It is the basis of all subsequent versions of the plays of Aeschylus.

There next came to light a parchment book containing seven plays by Sophocles, bound together with some plays of Aeschylus and a text by Apollonius of Rhodes. Soon thereafter a collection of the plays of Euripides turned up. These treasures did not long remain in manuscript. In 1502 Aldus printed an edition of the tragedies of Sophocles in the newly designed Greek Type. The following year he published the plays of Euripides, and in 1518 a first edition of Aeschylus. Other editions followed rapidly, and before long the Greek tragedies became readily available in bilingual format and, soon after, in the vernacular.

The thematic content of the Greek plays was not new to the Western world. The Senecan tragedies, modeled on the Greek, had been accessible to scholars throughout the Middle Ages, and were assiduously studied in schools as prime examples of Latin eloquence. Some time in the thirteenth century Nicholas Trivet published a commentary on the Senecan plays, in consequence of which a group of scholars at the university of Padua initiated the serious study of Roman tragedy. In the fourteenth century, apparently, tragedy was still considered a branch of poetry. It was not until the second half of the fifteenth century that the antique drama began to be enacted on the stage in schools and in theaters under courtly patronage.

The age was Latin. Since classic tragedy was generally considered to have reached its zenith in Rome, the Greek plays were seldom imitated. Long after the Greek tragedies were familiar in Western circles, Renaissance poets continued to write in imitation of Seneca. As late as 1543 the eminent author Giraldi insisted that Roman tragedy was vastly superior to the

Greek and that Seneca surpassed the Greeks in prudence, gravity, decorum, majesty, and skill in the use of sententious maxims—in short, in everything that was essential to the art of tragedy.[1] In Giraldi's opinion, which was widely shared, Seneca was the greatest of the tragic poets; he had brought the Greek drama to its perfection. And the *Ars Poetica* of Horace held the foremost place as a manual for dramatists.

Since Horace had fervently recommended the study of the Greek masterpieces, the Greek tragedies were generally accorded lip-service, but until the seventeenth century there is nothing to indicate that they exerted any considerable influence on the Renaissance theater. Until the close of the eighteenth century the *Poetics* of Aristotle and the Greek plays were seldom reprinted. The extraordinary interest they aroused in the following years may well be considered an aspect of the romantic revival of the classic tradition.

It is entirely possible that the existing body of Greek tragedy fairly represents the taste of the Attic audience of the fifth century, since a good proportion of the surviving plays is said to have won victories in the tragic contests. It is by no means certain. What was selected for preservation no doubt included the celebrated masterpieces, but ultimately the selection of manuscripts to be copied for transmission to posterity was in the hands, not of poets, but of librarians and schoolmasters. The result certainly reflects their idea of what was worth preserving, but whether it truly represents the great period of dramatic genius in Attica is, and is likely to remain, an open question.

The Greek tragedies were intended primarily for performance, but it is not likely that the authors considered their work ephemeral. Plays were often revived and reentered in competition, and probably copies were circulated to the trade. The texts that survived production were apparently no more stable than the playscripts of Shakespeare's time. Quintilian complains that in revivals actors altered their lines to suit their tastes. The precarious situation of the Greek masterpieces evidently caused some concern in official circles, for Plutarch notes that about 330 B.C. the archon Lycurgus ordered an official copy to be made of the plays of Aeschylus, Sophocles and Euripides for deposit in the civic archives. It appears that this text was inscribed in uncials on rolls of papyrus, like inscriptions in stone, without punctuation or separation of words and without any indication of the strophic structure of the odes. In the time of the second Ptolemy this manuscript was sent for reproduction to the library in Alexandria and, in the second century B.C., Aristophanes of Byzantium edited the text, divided the odes into cola, and added explanatory notes. By the second century A.D. the old Greek was no longer entirely comprehensible. At this time a selection of the ancient plays on comparable subjects was made for the use of students. This edition, several times reedited in Byzantium, was the basis of the manuscript that Aurispa brought to Italy in 1423.

In the following years scores of manuscripts of the Greek tragedies turned up in Europe, and there were many textual variants. In the course of time the texts have been carefully scrutinized and emended, scribal errors corrected, variants collocated and reconciled, so that the plays are now reconstituted in reasonable approximation to their original state. But even the most astute interpretation cannot restore the meaning of words that long ago lost their vitality. In the modern theater the Greek plays hold the stage with impressive authority, but what is done with them is, at best, conjectural. In spite of all that has been done by way of reconstruction, it is impossible to say with confidence what the ancient poets had in mind in composing tragedies or what the audience was expected to experience in the theater of Dionysus.

The life span of Greek tragedy can hardly be estimated. A fragmentary inscription of uncertain date lists the poets who won victories in the tragedic contests of the City Dionysia in the fifth century.[2] Aeschylus heads the list. It is known from an independent source that Aeschylus first competed for a prize in the year 499 and that he won his first victory in 484 at the age, presumably, of forty, the usual age for winning first victories. There is no doubt that tragedies were performed in Athens long before these dates. The annual contests were instituted by Pisistratus, it is said, about the year 535 B.C. The first victor was the legendary Thespis, the father of Greek drama, or at least its uncle. The names of a number of early dramatists have been preserved: Choerilus, Phrynicus, Pratinas. Next to nothing is known of their works. For all practical purposes Greek tragedy began with Aeschylus. It ended some time after the death of Euripides. It is impossible to say when.

Euripides died in 406, barely fifty years after the death of Aeschylus and just a year before or after the death of Sophocles. It appears, accordingly, that the great age of Greek tragedy was something less than a century. So far as the existing plays are concerned, its course extends from the time of the *Persians,* which Aeschylus presented in 472, to the date of Euripides's *Bacchae,* which was first produced, posthumously, in 405. A period of sixty-seven years. During this time and in the following century doubtless thousands of tragedies were written, and hundreds performed. The titles of some of these plays have come down to us, together with the names of their authors, and scholars have scraped together fragments that testify to the existence, over a period of at least two centuries, of a rich and varied dramatic literature. Of this only thirty-three examples have survived.

Of the seventy tragedies attributed to Aeschylus in the Medicean manuscript, we possess only seven. Alexandrian scholars apparently had knowledge of more than a hundred plays by Sophocles; seven have come down to our time. Euripides is said to have written some ninety tragedies; nineteen have survived. The larger figures border on the marvelous and are very likely exaggerated; nevertheless, we may very well wonder at the extraordinary productivity of these poets, none of whom, so far as is known, depended on the theater for his livelihood. Aeschylus is said to have won nineteen victories in the course of his life. His epitaph, which he composed himself, makes no mention of his prowess as a playwright. It proudly records his valor as a soldier on the field at Marathon.

THE GREEK THEATER

THE FESTIVAL OF Dionysus instituted by Pisistratus was enlivened by a series of contests in which the musical and poetic prowess of the Athenians was proudly displayed for the admiration of the world. On the first two days of the Dionysia choral groups competed for the prize. On the next three days plays were presented.

From the list of poets who offered tragedies for production, three contestants were chosen each year. To each of these entrants a chorus was assigned, and also the choregus who would finance the production. The choregus, a wealthy citizen, undertook to pay the chorus, provided its costumes, and saw to its training. The actors were paid by the state. The scenery and the flute player were provided by the author.

The chorus was a group of young men who could sing and dance. Much of the production would depend on their skill and experience, but it is not clear that they were at any time organized as professional performers. The actors, however, soon formed guilds. They were highly regarded and, as servants of Dionysus, were accorded special privileges, such as exemption from military service. The playwright directed the production, provided the music, and designed the spectacle. Apparently everyone was paid during the rehearsals. But they were all amateurs.

The plays were judged by a jury of ten citizens, representing the ten demes, and their judgment, if contested, was subject to official review. The victorious poet and his choregus were awarded prizes and much honor. The first prize was a goat.

The rites of the Ionian Dionysus were celebrated at the Lenaia, the festival of the new wine. This was held in the month of Gamelion, at the end of the year. At this festival, for a time, only comedies were performed.

In the spring, toward the end of March, in the month of Elaphebolion, the image of Dionysus Eleutherius was borne in procession from its temple in Athens to a shrine on the road to Eleutherae on the frontier of Boeotia. After elaborate ceremonies culminating in the sacrifice of a bull, the god was transported by torchlight to the theater near his temple on the southeast slope of the Acropolis. The image was then established on an altar dressed in the center of the dancing-place. It stood there throughout the duration of the festival.

On the second day the god was regaled with a contest of dithyrambs. Ten choruses took part, one from each of the ten tribes of Attica. The victor was awarded a bull. The contest of tragedies took place during the next three days. Each day one of the competing poets presented a group of three tragedies and a satyr play. Later in the day there was played a comedy.[1]

Presumably the performances began early in the day and went on until dusk. Few of the existing tragedies exceed fifteen hundred lines of verse, about half the length of an Elizabethan tragedy. It is hardly possible to estimate the tempo of the performance, but it is believed that the performances each day lasted ten hours, allowing two hours for intermissions and scene changes.[2] The theater of Dionysus accommodated a huge audience which included women and children. One marvels at its aptitude as well as its fortitude: in April a chill wind blows across the Acropolis.

Nothing is known of the standards of excellence which guided the judges appointed to appraise the competing tragedies. In the *Frogs* of Aristophanes, Dionysus agrees that the test of a tragedy is its moral worth and civic value.[3] But the actual judging of the works of Aeschylus and Euripides in the presence of the god involves a series of absurdities that was meant perhaps to parody the sort of thing that so often clouds critical judgment. Doubtless the volume of applause would put some pressure on the judges, and the quality of the production would probably have weighed as heavily in their estimation as the merit of the poetic composition. At any rate, it is hardly surprising that plays that are now considered outstanding masterpieces were passed over when they were first presented in favor of tragedies that have left no trace. The *Oedipus Tyrannus,* which Aristotle regarded as a supreme masterpiece, did not win a prize.

Apart from the ruins of the Greek theaters, most of which have been several times rebuilt, what we know regarding the physical character of the classic theater is largely derived from the testimony of the Greek lexicographer Julius Pollux, who lived in the second century A.D., and the fifth book of Vitruvius's *De Architectura,* a work compiled sometime about 25 B.C. A large number of vase paintings also appear to depict scenes from the classic theater, some of them in considerable detail.[4] But the paintings, while undoubtedly informative, leave something to be desired as documents; Vitruvius's work is late, terse, and exasperatingly obscure; and Pollux came very late on the Hellenic scene. Accordingly, much of what is said of the theater in the time of Pericles is guesswork, often brilliant, but strictly deductive.

The theater of Dionysus in Athens has undergone so many changes that it is all but impossible to reconstitute it imaginatively in its primitive form. Evidently there was a theater on this site long before the production of the *Persians* in 472. In the days of Pericles the theater consisted of a flat area adapted for dancing, circular in shape, and some sixty feet in diameter. This was called the orchestra. It was backed by a wooden shed called the skene, about twelve feet deep, with a wide practical door in the center, flanked by two smaller doors and surmounted by a substantial roof that could serve as an upper stage. The skene had projecting wings with passages, called parodoi, that led down to the orchestra. Between them, and in front of the skene was a narrow platform called the logeion, the speaking-place, some forty-five feet long, barely elevated above the orchestra. This was the actors' territory.

The hillside on the slope of the Acropolis made a natural amphitheater which served as an auditorium. Wooden benches were placed above the orchestra for the use of notables, and behind these sat the bulk of the audience, perhaps on bleachers set up for the occasion. This theater served the great age of tragedy. It was much altered before the middle of the fourth century, in the time of Lycurgus. The wooden stage building was rebuilt in stone, and the wooden seats were replaced by stepped seats of limestone. In late Hellenistic times the stage was elevated high above the orchestra, and the style of production necessarily changed radically. The theater was rebuilt once again in Roman times. Its ruins convey some idea of how it was in the days of Sophocles, but not without putting some strain on the imagination.

It has been estimated that the theater of Dionysus would accommodate some 15,000 spectators, perhaps more. The price of admission was nominal, one obol, and it might be remitted. Apparently no one was excluded, not even slaves. But obviously, the festival of Dionysus did not empty the city. It is said that in 431 B.C., at the outbreak of the Peloponnesian war, the population of Attica was in the neighborhood of 175,000 citizens, plus 30,000 aliens and 120,000 slaves, a total of some 325,000 people.[5] In the time of the *Oresteia,* in 458, the city of Athens itself held some 100,000. If the theater seated 15,000, only a fraction of the citizenry could have attended in any one day. The tragedic contests were doubtless of great national interest, but many people stayed home.

In the time of Aeschylus the logeion was raised a step or so above the orchestra, so that the principals and the chorus were not sharply separated, and the chorus could serve as an actor whenever that was required. The skene must have resembled a barn rather than a palace until Sophocles provided scenery, probably in the form of painted backcloths and screens. The central door of the skene must have been wide: in the *Eumenides* it is necessary to show a crowded interior, with Orestes seated on the omphalos, surrounded by the sleeping Furies, with Apollo and Hermes nearby. Tableaux of lesser magnitude were apparently managed by rolling out the eccyclema, a wagon stage with the set already arranged upon it. Something of the sort is certainly called for in the *Agamemnon* and the *Choephoroi,* and the fact that Aeschylus envisaged effects of this kind indicates that the scenic dispositions in his time were by no means as primitive as one might imagine. Nevertheless, the one item of stage machinery of which we can be sure in the Periclean theater is the crane, the mechane. This was a mast with a boom that was used to bring the gods down to earth or to swing contraptions like Trygaeus's dung beetle into the sky. Such a device would offer no difficulty to a nation of seafarers accustomed to handling nautical tackle, and everything indicates that for dramatic purposes it was indispensable.

Greek actors must have been highly skilled female impersonators. The earliest of the surviving tragedies centers on a female character, and Greek tragedy is full of interesting women. But Greek actors were men. Both actors and chorus wore masks, perhaps made of painted linen or wood, which served to identify and also to characterize the personages they represented. Pollux has a long list of masks carefully identified and classified by types, and some may be identified in vase-paintings and sculptures; the subject is bewildering.[6] In the time of Lycurgus, about 330 B.C., the tragic mask was embellished by what Pollux called an onkos, a lambda-shaped tower of hair which added height and gave the actor an unreal look, but it is likely that in the fifth century the tragic prosopon was meant to be convincingly realistic.

Actors in the time of Sophocles were richly costumed in sleeved tunics of embroidered cloth and colorful cloaks. They wore soft boots. The thick-soled clog, the cothurnus of tradition, apparently came in with the Hellenistic theater, possibly when the stage was raised above the dancing area. By all indications the theater of Dionysus was designed to make a colorful and opulent impression, and this would be consistent with the rich and highly ornate language of the tragic stage. Aristotle disparaged the use of spectacle as something alien to the art of poetry, but Greek tragedy made huge demands on the scenic artist. The plays are full of colorful processions. Horses and chariots are driven into the orchestra. Ghosts rise from the earth and from behind tombs. Gods descend from the sky. In *Prometheus Bound* Oceanus arrives on a winged steed, and his daughters appear in a flying omnibus. In the *Medea* the heroine makes her final exit in a sun chariot drawn by a dragon, and in the *Prometheus* and the *Bacchae* there are cataclysms and earthquakes and cosmic upheavals which would tax the ingenuity of a modern stage technician. It is impossible to say to what extent these effects were realized in the fifth century B.C. The scenic marvels suggested by the plays are certainly impressive, but the available apparatus was, so far as is known, extremely simple—some painted screens, a crane, a dolly on wheels, and perhaps the triangular plinths, the periaktoi, described by Vitruvius. If that was all the stage carpenter could provide, the Greek poet, like those of the Elizabethan theater, must have relied heavily on the imagination of the spectator.

THE ACTORS AND
THE CHORUS

G REEK TRAGEDY WAS arranged so that a play involving as many as a dozen characters could be performed by a company of three actors. Since the actors were masked, they were personally invisible; it was the masks, and not the actors who wore them, that represented the personages of the drama. The actor's function was simply to animate the mask and to give it voice and movement. He could not alter its expression. Consequently, the nature of the production was quite different from anything we are accustomed to experience in the modern theater. Greek tragedy was symbolic in a very special sense. It was a play of masks.

The sequence of episodes was designed to make it possible for the actor to slip out of one role and into another simply by going offstage to change his face while the chorus covered his absence with a performance of its own. At the end of the choricon the actor would then reappear in a new guise and play another role. While this system of play construction made it possible to produce plays at minimal cost, it evidently made heavy demands on the ingenuity of the playwright and the versatility of the actor. Thus, in the *Persians* the actor who impersonates Atossa is apparently expected to leave the stage and then reappear at the close of the stasimon in the guise of Xerxes and engage in a long musical threnos with the chorus. Few modern actors are capable of such feats.

Presumably the poet's thrift in handling his masks, and the actors' skill in animating them, would excite admiration on the part of a discriminating audience. Nothing survives to substantiate this supposition. We know that successful poets and their patrons were given prizes and acclaim, but few of the actors of the time have left more than a name.[1] In the modern theater actors are remembered long after plays are forgotten; perhaps this measures the difference between the ancient idea of theater and our own. In our theater, also, although the actor is expected to become the character he portrays, in practice this seldom happens. The more highly regarded the actor, the more visible he is likely to be. In the modern theater, as Maeterlinck long ago pointed out, the actor exists at the expense of the character; the character lives at the actor's cost: they are in some sense antagonists. They managed things differently in the ancient theater. The actor did not, and could not, exhibit himself. He displayed his virtuosity by disappearing behind the mask. As a person he was anonymous.

From the playwright's point of view the advantage of the play of masks was great, but there would be some inconvenience, undoubtedly, in the monolithic quality with which his characters were invested. The mask was imperturbable. No matter what it said, or heard, its expression did not change. Close up, the effect would be eerie. But since in the Athenian theater the spectators in the topmost galleries were seated some three hundred feet from the stage, it is arguable that the expression on the actor's face would hardly matter. In any case, character development was not an outstanding element in Greek drama. Characterological change was usually sudden and catastrophic, the result of a recognition or a sudden reversal of fortune, and could be manifested by a change of mask, as in the case of

Oedipus, or by a change in the actor's style of speech. Greek tragedy resounds with sounds of woe: masks could scream; they could not weep.

Aeschylus is said to have acted in his own plays. He was a notable innovator. In the *Persians* he has only four masks, and there are never more than two speakers on the stage. Fourteen years later, in the *Agamemnon,* he has six speaking parts. He has seven in the *Choephoroi,* and five in the *Eumenides.* These plays apparently were managed by two actors for, according to Aristotle, it was Sophocles who introduced the third actor. There are nevertheless few scenes in the tragedies of Sophocles in which three actors speak together. One cannot imagine that a conversation of this magnitude was beyond the capabilities of so skillful a dramatist. One is forced to conclude that a thrifty structure was considered a virtue in the Attic theater and that a good craftsman sought to achieve a strong effect with a strict economy of means.

It is entirely possible that the limitation of the acting company to three was a consequence of the size of the Attic theater and the scarcity of actors whose voices could command it. Judging by its present condition, the theater of Dionysus would certainly tax an actor's voice. But it seems more likely that the Greek dramatists accepted this limitation in the spirit that prompted the seventeenth-century playwrights to cherish the so-called Aristotelian rules with which the critics saddled them. The rules of the art, however arbitrary, posed a challenge which enabled the craftsman to show his skill. Evidently, he accepted them with pleasure.

In the fifth-century theater the chorus played an essential role. It was constantly visible and constantly in touch with both the principals and the audience. At times it served as a curtain. It could separate the audience from the play and concentrate its attention on itself. It could also bind the two together dramatically and emotionally. It was at times a participant in the action, an actor, as well as a mirror in which the action was reflected and brought into scale. It was also a musical instrument that accompanied and amplified the mood of the play and a dancer that absorbed and embodied its tensions. In addition it was occasionally, no doubt, something of a nuisance.

In the *Suppliants* of Aeschylus the chorus of Danaids is actually the protagonist. The action centers upon it, and since the maidens are fleeing from the fifty sons of Aegyptus, Pollux concluded that the tragic chorus at this time numbered fifty. The *Suppliants* was for a time thought to be the earliest of the tragedies of Aeschylus. A fragment of papyrus that has recently come to light, however, indicates that the play was first performed about the time of the *Oresteia* and is consequently among the last of the Aeschylean plays. In the *Agamemnon* the members of the chorus at a certain point speak in succession; there are twelve couplets, one for each of the choristers. The inference is that the tragic chorus at this time numbered twelve. This was, in all likelihood, the size of the chorus also in the *Suppliants.* Sophocles is said to have used a chorus of fifteen. There is nothing to indicate that the tragic chorus ever exceeded this number.

Since the formal pattern of Greek tragedy involved an alternation of acted episodes and interludes of choral song, the attention of the audience was constantly shifted from the orchestra to the logeion, an easy transition, since the two were contiguous. The musical interludes served a variety of uses. They were used to anticipate action and to comment on it, to cover time lapses, to heighten a suspense or to set a mood, to mark a climax and to discharge a tension. But whether the dramatic episodes were musically merged with the choral odes or crisply detached from them, the effect of the chorus was to make the audience aware from the moment the choristers entered the dancing-place that what was being done in the theater belonged to an order of reality that was other than the reality of the marketplace. Within the hallowed precinct of the theater it was permissible to give way to the emotions, and everything that was done there was directed to that end. In the theater of Dionysus one paid tribute to Dionysus.

In the absence of musical notation and choreographic directions it is hardly possible to imagine the dramatic effect of the choric passages on the development of the action. The only clue to the movements of the chorus is the rhythmic pattern of the ode to which it danced.

There were several types of choric song. The opening song, the parodos, was a moving-song, designed to take the chorus into its place in the orchestra. The stasimon was a standing-song, performed, it would appear, from a stationary position in the dancing-place. The kommos was an ensemble piece sung in alternate strophes by actor and chorus, usually at a climactic point in the action. The strophic system was purely rhythmic. Tragedy made no use of assonance or rhyme. In tragedy the typical ode was antistrophic in form. A rhythmical system, the strophe, was followed by a stanza of the same structure, the antistrophe. This was followed by a strophe of different texture, which was also repeated. The result was a sequence of strophic pairs, AA BB CC, and so on, of indefinite duration. The dithyramb was triadic in structure. A strophe was followed by an antistrophe of similar design, followed by a strophe of different structure, called the epode. After the epode was sung, the initial system was repeated. The sequence thus took the form AAB AAB AAB. Presumably these patterns, together with the character of the metrical system within them, give some idea of the movements of the singing chorus.

In tragedy the chorus often plays the part of an elderly commentator, but it is seldom the source of wisdom. As an actor the chorus is usually characterized as the common man, a being endowed with good sense and traditional beliefs but no unusual intelligence. The characterization is summary. In the *Ajax* and the *Philoctetes* it is a group of mariners, and its speech is lightly salted. In the *Rhesus* the chorus is composed of warriors; in the *Suppliants,* maidens in distress. In the *Prometheus* we have sea nymphs, and in the *Eumenides,* Furies. These are exceptional cases, and unusually colorful. In the main the chorus consists of elderly gentlemen or respectable women, the neighbors. Normally it is in sympathy with the tragic hero and thus serves to guide the sympathy of the audience, while at the same time it provides a neutral counterpoint to the high-pitched tones of the tragic actor.

When it is actively engaged in the action, as in the *Agamemnon,* the chorus is mainly represented by the exarch, but occasionally its members speak for themselves, and in some instances it is divided and at odds with itself. But in general it is characterized as a unit, a sane and relatively colorless presence which bridges the distance between the principals and the audience without positively identifying itself with either.

In the high time of tragedy the chorus provided a basis which served to measure the dramatic trajectory of the hero. Such plays as the *Ajax* afford an interesting interplay between the heroic character whose actions are capable of annoying the gods and a group of innocent citizens who are careful to annoy no one. But in time the chorus became simply a musical interlude. In the *Bacchae* the chorus of Lydian maidens is charming, but it serves no special purpose. It does perhaps provide a glimpse of the less terrifying aspect of the cruel god, but even so, it is after all no more than an embellishment, and it foreshadows a time when the tragic chorus would be regarded as a needless interruption of the dramatic narrative. It may well be that by the time of Aristotle's *Poetics* this had already happened. We read in the *Poetics:*

The chorus should be treated as one of the actors. It should be an integral part of the whole, and should participate in the action, not in the manner of Euripides, but as in the plays of Sophocles. In the plays of the later poets the songs are no more closely related to the plot than to the plot of some other tragedy. Nowadays they are even singing interpolated songs, a practice introduced by Agathon, yet what difference is there between singing interpolated songs and transferring a speech, or even a whole scene, from one play to another?[2]

PLAY CONSTRUCTION

A COMPARISON OF the innocent design of the *Suppliants* with the highly sophisticated pattern of the *Oedipus Tyrannus* and the careless structure of Euripides's *Orestes* suggests that the art of playmaking in the fifth century evolved from relatively archaic beginnings to an acme of developed craftsmanship and then declined into something like decadence. But it has not been possible to date the *Suppliants,* nobody knows when Sophocles first presented the *Oedipus,* and there is not much reason to disparage the structure of Euripides's later plays. There is actually nothing to indicate that in the fifth century tragedy evolved from humble beginnings to a height of masterly craftsmanship and then sank, somewhat abruptly, into the abyss. On the contrary, it is arguable that the simplicity of the *Suppliants* and the complexity of the *Antigone,* for example, depended less on the requirements of the audience than on the attitude of the poet with regard to the dramatic exigencies of his material. What evidence there is can best be gleaned by a collocation of some examples of playmaking in the course of the fifth century. One might begin with the *Persians.*

* * *

The *Persians* can be dated. It was first presented in 472, eight years after the battle of Salamis. It won a victory in that year; in the *Frogs,* produced in 405, Aristophanes has Aeschylus say that the play was his greatest work.

The play is set in Susa, at that time the Persian capital. The plot is extremely simple. The episodes are few. The narrative interest centers on the detailed recital of the messenger who describes the Persian disaster, a declamation of epic character. The description is vivid and perhaps accurate, but the list of Persian casualties is wholly fictitious, the Persian names are mouth-filling, but entirely imaginary, and even though the audience must have included a host of veterans with first-hand knowledge of the battle, the event is given the color of myth.

The *Persians* is a display of Athenian boastfulness, an early example of political propaganda, thinly disguised as a compassionate warning to the enemy to avoid future disasters by curbing its ambitions. There is no prologue. The chorus of elders enters the orchestra in a state of apprehension. Its members have been summoned by the regent queen, Atossa, who has been having bad dreams. The parodos is interrupted by the appearance of Atossa. She is in need of counsel. The chorus advises her to pray to the shade of the great Darius, her husband, before whose tomb in the temple they are assembled. She inquires about Athens, the enemy, of which so far she knows nothing. She is told it is a rich city, a powerful democracy, far away in Greece. At this point the messenger arrives.

He is the bearer of evil tidings. The Persian army is in ruins. A Greek deceived Xerxes into making the fatal maneuver that cost him his fleet. The Greeks then massacred his land forces on the island of Salamis. What is left of the Persian army has been forced to retreat northward through Thrace under appalling conditions.

After much lamentation Atossa goes to make sacrifices to the Persian dead, while the chorus sings a stasimon. Then Atossa returns, in mourning, with liquid offerings to the shade of Darius—milk, water, honey, oil and wine. The chorus prays to Hermes to let the great king tell them what the future holds for Persia. When the ghost appears, Atossa informs it of the disaster that has befallen their son Xerxes. Darius says that Xerxes was guilty of hubris in bridging the Hellespont to cross over into Greece and has consequently incurred nemesis. He then gives the chorus an instructive summary of Persian history and advises it not to bother the Greeks in future. In the end Atossa is told to prepare new clothes for Xerxes, who is on his way home. After that, Darius vanishes.

Atossa withdraws and is not seen again. The chorus sings of the conquests of Darius. And now Xerxes appears. He is in rags and unattended. He sings a kommos with the chorus, a discordant ode full of sounds of woe, in the course of which the dead Persian chiefs are numbered, this time by the chorus, with convincing names which are unknown to history. In the end, Xerxes asks to be led to the palace, all the time wailing piteously. The chorus files out with him, singing the exodos.

The *Persians* can be played acceptably by two actors and the chorus. It has no scene changes and no need of scenery. It is, in the main, a musical lamentation, a display of sympathy, but it is most improbable that it was meant to evoke a measure of compassion for the beaten enemy. Xerxes might well be considered a tragic figure, but in fact his distress is highly exaggerated. His armies were in fact still formidable, and the character was hardly designed to elicit the sympathy of an audience which still had reason to fear him. On the contrary, it would seem that the play was intended to flatter the Athenians and to reassure them with regard to the eastern threat. It was intended, evidently, not to arouse pity, but to assuage fear.

The *Persians* is the only existing Greek tragedy that deals with a historical event. Its tone is elegiacal rather than dramatic, but it has all the formal characteristics of the later drama. Thus, at the point where it first comes into history, Greek tragedy appears as a mature and highly developed art form, simple, but in no way archaic.

* * *

The *Oresteia* can also be dated. It won a victory in 458, four-teen years after the *Persians*. Aeschylus was at that time seventy and, judging by this work, at the very peak of his powers. The *Oresteia* binds together thematically the terminal events of the myth of the house of Atreus—the murder of Agamemnon and the revenge of Orestes, with his acquittal by the grace of god and the Athenian people. It is a trilogy. Unlike the *Persians*, it is forceful and active.

The only comparable work we possess is Sophocles's triad of Theban plays. These were not offered as a trilogy. The three plays, the *Antigone*, the *Oedipus Tyrannus* and the *Oedipus Coloneus*, were written at widely separated intervals and were never, so far as is known, played together. The *Prometheus Bound*, usually attributed to Aeschylus, is said to be the first tragedy of a trilogy entitled the *Promethea*, the *Suppliants* is perhaps the initial play of a trilogy called *The Danaids*, and *The Septem* is supposedly the last play of a trilogy based on the Theban cycle. But whatever can be said of these trilogies rests largely on conjecture. All that is known with regard to the nature of trilogies depends on the *Oresteia*.

The *Oresteia* is the work of a master. The pace is majestic. The diction is fluid and elaborately high-sounding. Yet the action, once it starts, is swift and managed with economy and power. Aeschylus did not permit the spatial and temporal limi-tations of the theater to affect the scope of his drama. The action in each of the three plays moves freely in space and time, and while each play is focused on a single happening, the trilogy not only synthesizes the themes, but carries them to a politically useful conclusion.

The *Agamemnon* opens in Argos some hours after the fall of Troy. It ends, presumably, some weeks later. The author did not assume that his audience was entirely familiar with the myth. Consequently he provided the chorus with long expository passages in the course of which all the motives relating to the murder of Agamemnon are set forth, so that by the end of the play everything has been recalled that is relevant to the action. The *Agamemnon* is, as a result, some six hundred lines longer than the other two tragedies of the trilogy. If these passages were sung by the full chorus, one wonders how clearly their content was conveyed.

This play fairly represents the design of Greek tragedy at the height of its development. The prologos is spoken before the action starts, while the orchestra is empty. A single actor is seen, perched on the roof of the skene. He represents the lookout posted by Clytemnestra on the tower of the citadel of Mycenae to watch for the beacon which will announce the fall of Troy in the tenth year of the siege. There is a glow on the horizon. It is the long-awaited signal. He awakens the city.

As the chorus of elders enters the orchestra, the parodos recalls the story of the Trojan expedition and the sacrifice of Iphigenia at Aulis. And now Clytemnestra appears with news of the fall of Troy. The old men are neither altogether convinced nor altogether jubilant. Victory, they sing, has its dangers:

> Glory in excess invites misfortune. It is the high peak
> that is struck by the bolt from the sky. My choice is the
> sort of success that does not excite envy. Let me not be
> a destroyer of cities.[1]

The elders speak in succession, expressing their apprehension and their distrust of women's words and women's rule. A herald puts an end to their uncertainties; he confirms Clytemnestra's news and announces the arrival of Agamemnon, who, alone of all the Achaeans, has succeeded in bringing his ship safely to the shores of Greece.

The elders are restrained in their rejoicing. They revile Helen for the evil she has caused. At the end of the stasimon there is heard the sound of hooves, and Agamemnon drives up in his chariot along with Cassandra, his young captive. After giving solemn thanks to the gods of the city and announcing his intention of setting its affairs in order, he turns at last to Clytemnestra. She speaks of her love, her fears for his safety, and her ten years of loneliness. Then she invites him to walk to the palace on the rich cloths she has spread on the ground for his passage. Agamemnon cuts short her praises. He declines to tread on the costly cloths:

> Such honors become the gods. For a mortal to tread on such rich things is to give rise to apprehension. I bid you honor me as a man, not as a god.[2]

But Clytemnestra insists, and after a long stichomythic interchange, Agamemnon accedes to her wishes:

> Very well, since you wish it, let someone quickly loose my sandals, these slaves I tread on, but as I crush these textures red with dyes from the sea, may no god look down on me with jealousy.[3]

He enters the palace. But when the queen comes out to lead Cassandra into the house, Cassandra stands stubborn and silent in her chariot. It is only when Clytemnestra once again leaves the stage that Cassandra descends. Left alone with the chorus, she becomes voluble. Apollo, she tells the elders, has cast her off, but she retains the power of prophecy and is able to foretell the death of Agamemnon and her own death. The old men understand nothing of this, but they are frightened. Cassandra enters the house. In a moment we hear Agamemnon's death-cry. The chorus breaks apart. Each man cries out in turn, and amid the hubbub of voices, the palace gates fly open, and Clytemnestra is seen standing over the corpses of Agamemnon and Cassandra.

And now Clytemnestra speaks her mind. The death of Agamemnon, she says, was planned long ago in reprisal for the murder of her daughter Iphigenia. But the chorus does not justify her. It threatens to drive her from the city. She has a further excuse. It was not she, she says, that struck down her husband, but the ghost of Thyestes:

> It was the old implacable avenger in the semblance of the wife of this dead man that struck him down in requital for the deed of Atreus, the grim banqueter, taking this life in payment for the lives of the slaughtered children.

The old men will not absolve her:

> So long as Zeus abides the law is fixed: the doer must pay for what is done.

Clytemnestra answers that she is ready to pay the blood price, provided that will serve to close her account with the dead:

> Now I make this vow to the spirit that haunts the house of Pleisthenes: However high the price of this my deed, I will endure the cost. Only let him go and trouble us no more. Let him avenge the blood guilt in the house of another.[4]

At this point Aegisthus appears. His tone is haughty. He assumes responsibility for the death of Agamemnon, which, he says, he himself planned. The chorus threatens to stone him. He summons his guards. Swords are drawn. But Clytemnestra averts the brawl and dismisses the elders. They pray for the coming of Orestes; then in sullen silence they depart.

In this play the chorus is a principal actor, and therefore quite carefully characterized. It is by turns mistrustful, apprehensive, skeptical, puzzled and in the end defiant. The other characters are carefully portrayed. Clytemnestra is regal, dangerous and devious. Agamemnon is pompous. Cassandra is pathetic and mysterious. The moral issue is left open. As the play is conceived, each of the characters has a plausible justification for his actions, but all are at fault. Aeschylus injected from the outset the issue which he intended to resolve at the end of the trilogy. The conflict of masculine and feminine authority, which is the subject of the first stasimon, is extended far beyond the limits of a family feud. It becomes a cosmic issue which is resolved in the reconciliation of the ancient order typified by the Furies and the new order instituted by Zeus. In the meantime it is made clear that past wrongs can be righted only by future wrongs. The *Agamemnon* concludes in a bitter altercation which leaves the outcome in suspense. There is no resolution.

* * *

The *Choephoroi* necessitates a scene change. It begins with Orestes and his friend Pylades at the tomb of Agamemnon somewhere in the vicinity of the palace. It is significant that while Agamemnon figures only briefly in the play that bears his name and is wholly absent from its sequel, his spirit pervades the action of the *Choephoroi* so poignantly that it seems that he alone is the motivating force of what follows. In consequence the *Choephoroi* has an unearthly quality which leads quite naturally into the supernatural atmosphere of the *Eumenides*. The *Oresteia* is, on the whole, a ghost story.

There is no clue to the length of time that separates the one play from the other. Evidently Aeschylus had no interest in fixing temporal values beyond what was strictly necessary to collocate the vital scenes of his action. In the *Agamemnon* the action covers a period of days or perhaps weeks. The *Choephoroi* might take place in an hour.

In the prologue Orestes reverently invokes his father's spirit and lays a lock of hair on the tomb. The two friends then hide while a procession of slave women, led by Electra, files into the orchestra, bearing offerings to appease the ghost of the dead king. Clytemnestra has had a foreboding dream. Electra, however, has no idea of calming the angry spirit. On the contrary, she asks Hermes to inflame the ire of the spirits that watch over the house. It is then that she sees the lock of hair and the footprints around the tomb. Yet when Orestes appears, she is slow to acknowledge his identity. When at last she does, he tells her that, in obedience to the orders of Apollo, he has come to kill his mother. The chorus of women commends his mission:

> The spirit of justice clamors for the settlement of the debt. Blood must be paid for with blood. Whoever acts must endure the consequences. So speaks the ancient wisdom.[5]

The chorus knows what is at work in the house of Atreus. It tells Orestes:

> Child, although the fire with its teeth tears apart the body it cannot conquer the spirit's will. Though the man is dead, his anger lives.[6]

Electra, Orestes, and the chorus then sing in concert, inter-
mingling their voices in alternate strophes, invoking the spirits
of the dead. The poet was evidently worried about the length
of the kommos, for the chorus tells Orestes:

> Nobody can find fault with the long-drawn prayer
> which gives the unhonored grave its due. Do now what
> must be done.[7]

The action accelerates. Orestes proposes to gain access to
the house by pretending that he and Pylades are travelers from
Phocis. He leaves the stage, and the chorus covers his absence
with a stasimon which recalls the deeds of various treacherous
women. Then Orestes and Pylades reappear. They knock at the
palace gate. Clytemnestra welcomes them and is told that
Orestes is dead. She ushers her guests into the house. For a
moment the stage is empty. Then the old nurse Cilissa comes
out to fetch Aegisthus. On the way, she pauses to deliver a
touching speech about how she cared for Orestes when he was
a child. The chorus asks her to tell Aegisthus to come un-
guarded, and again it invokes the aid of the gods. Aegisthus
enters the house. A moment later a servant comes out to announce his death. Clytemnestra rushes out of the women's
wing. She calls for an axe, but she has no time to defend herself.
Orestes and Pylades run at her with drawn swords. Orestes
hesitates, and now for the first time Pylades speaks. It is better,
he says, to incur the hatred of men than to provoke the anger
of the gods. They drag Clytemnestra into the house. The chorus
sings. Then the gates open and Orestes displays the dead bod-
ies lying on the blood-stained net in which Agamemnon was
entangled when he died. They sing a kommos. Then come the
Furies ("the hell-hounds of the mother's curse"), and with

these creatures in pursuit, Orestes sets out for Delphi to be purified. The play ends, like the *Agamemnon,* with a question:

> Where now shall all this end? Where shall the fury of
> fate at last be calmed and stilled?[8]

The question introduces the last play of the trilogy.

* * *

The *Choephoroi* serves admirably as a transition between the two planes on which the drama of Orestes is played. The *Agamemnon* takes place in the world of men. In the *Choephoroi* supernatural forces are activated and ultimately become visible. In the *Eumenides* the avenging powers of the cosmos take on the solidity of characters, and their quarrel over the sin of Orestes goes far beyond the question of his fate. The agon debates a cosmic issue.

The *Eumenides* is played in two scenes which are widely separated in place and time. It has two actions, related but quite distinct. The one concerns the story of Orestes. The other represents the reconciliation of two orders of justice and of the powers that administer them, the retributive and the judicial. Blind retribution is personified by the Furies; the judicial function is embodied in the court of Athenian citizens convened by Athene. When the reconciliation takes place, the Furies are miraculously transformed into benign goddesses who will henceforth serve to implement the new order even though its decisions are no longer in their hands. Thus, justice becomes a civic concern, dependent on the judgment of male citizens under the tutelage of the goddess of wisdom, who is also the patroness of the city.

The prologue of the *Eumenides* takes place at Delphi. The

Pythia, after a solemn invocation, enters the sacred shrine. She comes out at once, appalled at the scene within. The gates of the temple open. Orestes is revealed seated on the omphalos, attended by Apollo and Hermes and surrounded by the Furies, who have been lulled to sleep. Apollo speaks; he formally assumes responsibility for the matricide and assures Orestes of his support. He then sends him off to Athens, where the goddess will look after him.

When Orestes and Hermes have gone, the ghost of Clytemnestra awakens the Erinyes. They blame Apollo for aiding Orestes, whom it is their duty to punish since the murder of kindred is their special concern. The murder of Agamemnon does not interest them for, in their opinion, mother and son are blood-related but husband and wife are not. Apollo disagrees. Marriage, he says, is a sacred bond, sanctified by nature and honored by the example of Zeus and Hera. The Furies are not impressed. They set off in pursuit of Orestes.

The scene changes. It is now the temple of Pallas in Athens. Orestes is revealed kneeling as a suppliant at the foot of the statue of the goddess. The chorus of Furies comes in, questing like hounds following the scent of blood. Their ode describes the sacred mission with which Zeus and Apollo are interfering. Athene appears. The Furies put their case in her hands, and she initiates the trial of Orestes. He denies nothing. He acted, he says, at the command of Apollo. Athene cannot ignore the Furies' claim. She proposes to convene a court of Athenians to decide the issue and departs to select the jury. When she returns, she orders the public to be summoned, and the trial begins again. The Furies accuse Orestes of matricide, for which the penalty is death. But Apollo, speaking with the authority of Zeus, denies that the murder of Clytemnestra violated the blood-bond. Mothers and sons are not, he declares, blood-related:

> The woman is not the parent of her so-called child, but
> only the nurse of the seed newly planted in her. The
> man who mounts her is the parent. She is a stranger to
> the stranger's seed she nourishes.[9]

Athene then asks the judges to cast their ballots, while she
herself votes openly for acquittal. When the votes are counted,
they are found to be equally divided, and pursuant to custom,
Orestes is set free. He leaves the court gratefully, engaging the
Argives to eternal alliance with Athens.

The Furies, however, are outraged, and threaten to vent
their wrath on the land. But Athene first threatens them with
the might of Zeus, then placates them by offering them a share
of divine power and worship. They accept her offer of a shrine
hard by the temple of Erectheus, and the play ends with a
torchlight procession as the new patronesses of the city are
escorted to their home under the mount of Ares. The conclusion is a scene of universal rejoicing.

* * *

Sophocles's *Antigone* can be dated confidently about the year
442, sixteen years after the production of the *Oresteia,* and
only thirty years after the date of the *Persians.* The first of the
three plays which Sophocles drew from the Theban cycle, it
dramatizes an incident which took place long after the exile of
Oedipus and some time before his death and transfiguration at
Colonus.

The *Antigone* was written early in Sophocles's long career
in the theater. The plot is complex and subject to various interpretations, none of them altogether satisfying. It deals with the
subject of civil disobedience, but it is in no sense a thesis play.
It is above all a play of character. It depicts the collision of two
headstrong people, each of whom is convinced of the rightness
of his cause. The result is fatal for both.

It is tempting to discern in this tragedy the elements of the dramatic scheme of which Seneca's *Octavia* became the outstanding example, the play of the cruel tyrant and the beautiful and innocent victim. Sophocles doubtless designed his plot so as to solicit sympathy for Antigone. But in the end the hapless tyrant becomes an object of pity, and the play is tragic in portraying two characters trapped by what they honestly consider to be their duty but is in reality their pride.

The *Antigone* poses also a social problem. This involves the conflict of the interests of the clan with the interests of the state, and thus in some sense it reflects a political situation which in the time of Sophocles was not yet entirely resolved. In his celebrated analysis of this tragedy Hegel developed the dialectical structure in which Ibsen found a basis for modern tragedy. But Sophocles does not seem to have designed his play in terms of a clash of antitheses. Essentially the play is a love story.

The prologue is expository. In the course of a dialogue between Antigone and her sister Ismene the audience learns that Eteocles and Polyneices, the twin sons of Oedipus, have just killed one another in the war of the succession. The new king, Creon, has forbidden the burial of Polyneices. Antigone, his sister, has resolved to disobey this edict. The chorus of Theban elders then comes in, singing joyfully of the lifting of the siege. At the end of the parodos, Creon appears. He reminds the chorus very forcefully that the body of Polyneices must be left in the open to rot. But now a frightened guard runs in. He reports that the corpse of Polyneices has already been buried. Creon is furious. He threatens to hang the elders unless they produce the culprit. The chorus now sings, somewhat inappropriately, an ode extolling the race of men. The guard then drags in Antigone.

When Creon reproaches the girl for breaking his law, Antigone urges the primacy of the law of nature over the decrees of kings. The chorus praises her piety and her courage, but

Creon threatens to put both sisters to death. He speaks of Polyneices as an enemy of the state and an object of national hatred. Antigone replies that she has no hatred. She has only love. The chorus sings of the curse on the house of Labdacus:

> No generation can clear its progeny of guilt. A god will strike. There is no escape. And now the light goes out for the house of Oedipus, and the bloody knife, driven by foolish speech and foolish anger, cuts the last root. . . . For now, and in time to come, as in the past, one law holds good: when greatness comes it brings a curse.[10]

At this point Haemon enters. He was to have married Antigone, and he is outraged by his father's rash decision. But Creon tells him:

> The man the state appoints to power must have unquestioning obedience in all things, great and small, in just things and also in things unjust.[11]

The greatest danger to an orderly administration, he says, is disobedience. In this respect women are a nuisance. The daughters of Oedipus pose a special problem:

> If I must fall from power, far better to fall by the hand of a man. No one shall have cause to call me weaker than a woman.[12]

The chorus sides with Creon. But Haemon tells his father that public opinion is against him. The Thebans think that Antigone has acted nobly. There is an angry dispute in stichomythic verse, after which Haemon flings off in a fury, and Creon orders Antigone to be immured in a cave and left there to die. The chorus sings of love and its dangers:

love, unconquered in battle, love who wastes our
wealth, you dwell in the bloom of a young girl's cheek,
you ride the seas and range the desert. The immortal
gods cannot avoid your power, nor can man whose life
is but a day. And when you come you bring madness
with you.[13]

Antigone is led out to die. She sings with the chorus, which
praises her fortitude but blames her arrogance. She would not
have laid down her life for a husband, she says, nor for her
children, for these might be replaced, but a brother is irreplace-
able. She is then led away, and the chorus recalls the sad fate
of Danaë, Cleopatra and other legendary ladies who suffered
unjust punishment. At this juncture blind Tiresias appears. The
gods are angry, he tells Creon. Their altars are polluted. The
body of Polyneices must at all costs be laid in the earth. There
is an angry altercation in which Tiresias is, as usual, accused of
accepting bribes. In the end, Creon grows fearful, and now the
chorus advises him to release Antigone while there is time. He
hurries off to save her. But it is too late. A messenger describes
the death of Antigone and Haemon's suicide. Creon's wife,
Eurydice, hitherto mute, enters the house silently when she
hears the news. Creon comes in with the body of his son. He
blames his misfortune on the gods:

It was a god that struck me down and brought disaster
on my head. He drove me to wild and evil ways![14]

But there is more: a messenger announces that Eurydice has
killed herself, cursing her husband. The palace gates open, and
her body is displayed. Creon hopes for a speedy death and is
led into the house. The chorus sings the exodos:

Happiness depends on wisdom. The gods must ever
have their due. Proud words proudly uttered are fol-

43

lowed always by great blows from above. And so it is
that wisdom comes with age.[15]

The plot of the *Antigone* in some sense foreshadows the
scheme of Euripides's *Hippolytus*. Antigone is used by the gods
as an instrument for the destruction of Creon. For their purposes, she is expendable, and with her death the gods make a
clean sweep of the house of Labdacus. This is apparently their
object. The education of Creon comes somewhat late in his life,
but it serves as an example to others. Creon believes he is acting
in the interests of the state he has newly been appointed to
govern. There is a party in opposition. He is fearful and jealous
of his authority; consequently his actions are in every way excessive. The parallel to the behavior of Oedipus in the first
scenes of the *Tyrannus* seems clear: both men are frightened.
When Creon comes to his senses, however, he believes he was
visited by Ate. The chorus concurs:

It was a wise man who said, to one doomed by the
gods, the bad seems good.[16]

In a plot conceived along these lines, character portrayal is an
essential element, and indeed, with this play Sophocles seems
to have broken new ground with respect to characterization.
Here, seemingly for the first time, the plot is devised so as to
show the characters in high relief. The effect is memorable.

The plot is simple. The *Antigone* has eight masks and is
easily played by three actors. It takes place in a single day in a
single setting and develops a single action. After the prologue
and the parodos it has six episodes separated by five choric
passages. The exodos is brief and may be taken as a moral
summation of the narrative. The action takes place mainly offstage. What is represented is a series of spirited confrontations.
The rest is described in epic style by a messenger. It is a tech-

nique which Sophocles brought to its perfection in the *Oedipus Tyrannus* some fifteen years later.

* * *

The *Bacchae* of Euripides shows no sign of decadence, but its structure is distinctly different from the firm, logical sequence of the *Antigone* and the *Oedipus.* The *Bacchae* was produced posthumously, in 406, a half-century after the *Ajax* and a year before the production of the *Oedipus Coloneus* in 405. It makes an impression totally unlike that of the *Antigone* or the *Ajax,* yet its theme is much the same. All three plays demonstrate the unpleasant consequences of annoying the powers that control the lives of men.

In the *Bacchae* Pentheus is a well-established ruler. He is a haughty and self-confident young man who is determined to defend his city, Thebes, against the invasion of an effeminate foreign cult. But Pentheus is no more a match for Dionysus than is Ajax for Athene. His downfall is vivid. Whereas in the *Ajax* we do not see the clouding of Ajax's mind by Athene, only its result, in the *Bacchae* the possession of the soul of Pentheus is depicted in considerable detail.

This scene is altogether unique in Greek tragedy and must have been difficult to play. Evidently by the end of the century the technical capability of the Greek theater had developed to the point where things could be done on the stage which fifty years before no dramatist had ventured to attempt.

The *Bacchae* has eight masks, a chorus of maenads and a host of supernumerary characters. It is a densely populated play and was conceived as an elaborate spectacle. It won a victory, but the text has not been well preserved. Modern editions are based on a single manuscript which lacks a vital page and has been the subject of much discussion. But the major outlines of the action are clear. The play is set in Thebes in the time of Cadmus. The myth on which the plot is grounded concerns the love of Zeus for Semele, Cadmus's daughter, consumed by lightning in the act of conceiving Dionysus. But Euripides did not deal with the myth of the twice-born god in this play. The *Bacchae* is about the homecoming of Dionysus.

The plot includes a prologue, six episodes, and two very long narrative recitals spoken by a messenger. In the prologue the god addresses the audience directly. He is newly arrived in Thebes, having come from the east, from Lydia, to manifest his power in the city of his birth and to teach the Hellenes his mysteries. Thebes has scorned him, however, and in anger Dionysus has punished the Thebans by infecting their women with his frenzy. They are running wild on the slopes of Mount Cithaeron. Cadmus has abdicated in favor of young Pentheus, and since Pentheus refuses to honor the god, Dionysus is about to teach him a lesson. He calls his women together. We do not see him again until the end of the play.

The chorus of Lydian women enters singing a hymn in honor of their god. Then blind Tiresias appears. He is in Bacchic attire and is joined by Cadmus. Hand in hand the old men set out for the mountain, wearing fawn skins and ivy, singing and dancing as if suddenly rejuvenated. They are stopped by Pentheus and his guards. When Tiresias counsels him to welcome the Lydian stranger, Pentheus angrily orders his men to destroy the prophet's shrine. The two old men then trot off, singing, while the chorus intones a hymn to Bacchus, who brings joy to his followers and pain to those who scorn him.

The guards bring in the Lydian. Pentheus subjects him to a brutal interrogation, cuts off his long hair, and has him bound and shut up in the stables. Suddenly a mysterious voice is heard in the house. The walls shake, there are flames, the palace collapses, the chorus falls prostrate in fear, and the stranger reappears, free of his bonds. And now a Messenger runs in with news that the maddened women on the mountain are tearing sheep apart and destroying villages. The stranger offers to lead Pentheus to the mountain so that he can see for himself what the women are doing. At first Pentheus indignantly refuses, but after some mysterious talk he agrees. The chorus sings again of the beauty of nature and the joy of life. Meanwhile it appears that Dionysus has driven Pentheus mad. Pentheus comes out of the palace dressed as a Bacchante, in woman's finery, and while the chorus sings, the stranger parades his victim through the city to the enchanted mountain.

When the choral ode is finished, the Messenger relates in detail how Pentheus was plucked down from his perch in a tree and torn apart by the maddened women. The chorus exults in the god's revenge, but when Agave marches in bearing her son's head on the end of her wand, the maidens are moved to lament her case. Cadmus then appears with the vestiges of his grandson. Agave regains her wits. There is a scene of general lamentation, at the end of which Dionysus appears in a cloud. He has, he says, now carried out the will of Zeus, and he orders Cadmus and Agave into a long and painful exile. The chorus concludes with Euripides's canonical reference to the unexpected outcome of his play:

> What was most expected has not happened. For that which was unexpected the gods have found a way. Such was the end of this story.

The *Bacchae* is remarkable for the beauty of its lyrics, but essentially it is a play of horror. It celebrates the dual nature of the god who best represents the two sides of man, the joy of his nature and its bestiality, in a way that has no parallel in the history of the drama. With this play the great age of tragedy abruptly ends. The interval that separates its production from that of the *Persians,* some threescore and seven years in all, is hardly comparable to the single generation that saw the development of English drama from Preston's *Cambises* to Shakespeare's *Coriolanus*. But the magnitude of the achievement in each case is truly a cause for wonder. In the years between the time of Preston and the age of Shakespeare there are, no doubt, some plays of note, but there is nothing to prepare us for the sudden emergence of *Romeo and Juliet* and, some six years later, *Hamlet*, so we have reason to regard Shakespeare as something in the nature of a miracle. However, the Greek theater from the time of Aeschylus holds no such surprises. There is certainly some development in plot construction and scenic display but, judging by the *Frogs*, nothing of sufficient importance to impress even so astute a critic as Dionysus. What is startling in the Greek theater is not the rapidity of its progress, but the abruptness of its end.

THE *POETICS*

A SIDE FROM THE surviving manuscripts and the glosses with which the scholiasts embellished them, our only reliable source of information with regard to the Greek tragedies is the *Poetics* of Aristotle.

This little book seems to have aroused scant interest in antiquity. It is not mentioned by Horace, Longinus, or Quintilian. It was certainly known in the Middle Ages, but seldom quoted. A version of the Greek text was translated into Syriac, later into Arabic, and sometime in the twelfth century Averroes made an abridged version of the latter text. It had some currency, but Averroes had no idea of theater and was seemingly unaware that tragedy was meant to be acted. His Arabic was translated into Latin in the course of the thirteenth century. Petrarch seems to have heard of the *Poetics,* but it was known neither to Dante nor to Boccaccio.

In 1498 Giorgio Valla published a version of the *Poetics* in Latin. Ten years later Aldus printed a text in Greek. In 1529 Giangiorgio Trissino wrote an extensive paraphrase, and some years later Alessandro de' Pazzi published a good Latin translation at the Aldine press. It was not, however, until 1548, when Francesco Robortelli published his *In librum Aristotelis de arte poetica explicationes,* that the *Poetics* aroused serious critical interest. The following year Segni brought out a translation in Italian; in 1570 Castelvetro's Italian *Poetica* was printed in Vienna, and six years later in Basel. A number of learned commentators now hastened to put their idea of the *Poetics* before the public. A generation after Pazzi's translation Aristotle's little treatise was firmly established as the prime classical authority on the art of poetry.

The *Poetics* is not a formal discourse. It is a synopsis intended perhaps as notes for a lecture or as the outline for a treatise that was never written. The various translations and interpretations that have appeared from the time of Trissino to that of Butcher, Bywater, Fyfe, Margoliouth, Gilbert, and other eminent authorities, are reconstitutions of a text that even in the most capable hands remains doubtful. Aristotle's book does much to describe the dramatic practice of his time, but that was not its primary purpose. Its aim was to define a method of playmaking that would best serve the ends of tragedy as Aristotle understood them. On this head there was evidently no general agreement. The *Poetics* consequently is not primarily concerned with what was actually done in the development of the art, but with what should be done in its furtherance. It is a book of instruction, a manual for playwrights, and only incidentally a critical work.

It is also, in some sense, a defense of poetry. At the end of the discussion in the Tenth Book of the *Republic* Plato invites the lovers of poetry, even if they are not poets, to show that poetry is not only enjoyable in itself, but also helpful to society and the life of man.[1] It is likely that in writing the *Poetics* Aristotle had it in mind to take up Plato's challenge. The *Poetics,* indeed, is the work not of a poet, but of a lover of poetry. Aristotle was a naturalist engaged in a compendious survey of the world. Since he considered the world to be rationally conceived and therefore knowable through logical analysis, he classified the manifestations of nature in terms of their causes and consequences, their origin, structure and reason for being. In the *Poetics*, accordingly, poetry is analyzed by methods analogous to those which served in the classification and description of all physical phenomena.

Art, in Aristotle's opinion, is mimetic. It mirrors nature and is pleasurable because mimicry is fun. It is edifying insofar as it imitates life, not in its accidental and ephemeral aspect, but in its universal and essential character. Tragedy is the imitation of an action, a happening. But unlike history, it represents not what is said to have taken place, but what might or should have happened in order to produce the effect which it is the aim of tragedy to produce. This aim is the provocation of fear and pity—the tragic effect. On this assumption the whole of the *Poetics* hangs.

The difference between poetry and history is thus a matter of the viewpoint—the distance between the poetic imitation in each case and the actual. Historical narratives have their truth—a matter of accuracy in reporting fact. But the truth of poetry depends on the skill of the poet in creating a believable fantasy. In Aristotle's view what happens in reality need be neither necessary nor probable. It is credible because it happened. But in order to have poetic truth, the happenings of myth must be arranged in a necessary and probable sequence. Tragedy is not a work of nature. It is a work of art.

Aristotle was evidently an assiduous theatergoer, but he was not a man of the theater. The *Poetics* is mainly concerned with literary matters. It does not deal seriously with any aspect of the drama other than the composition of the text. In Aristotle's opinion, tragedy differs from epic poetry mainly in its form and scope: since it is intended for performance by actors, tragedy is limited by the exigencies of the theater, whereas the epic, designed for declamation by an elocutionist, has no special limitations. Both are varieties of narrative poetry, "imitations of serious actions in a grand style of verse," and therefore governed by the same general principles; Aristotle evidently saw no essential distinction between them as poetry.[2]

The *Poetics* summed up an era in the development of the drama, but there is nothing to indicate that Aristotle was aware of the decline of tragedy in his time. It was probably written in the year 330, about the time when Lycurgus rebuilt the theater of Dionysus in stone, some seventy years after the death of the last two great tragic poets. At this time only comedy was a vital art, but the *Poetics* deals mainly with tragedy. The discussion of comedy that was apparently intended to follow it either was never written or has completely disappeared.

In the *Poetics* tragedy is treated as an organism developing naturally in accordance with its essential nature. Brief consideration is given to its origin, its species, the scope of its evolution, and its function in the order of things, its final cause. After a careful and precise definition, the constituent elements of tragedy are enumerated and analyzed, and helpful hints are provided for those who desire to excel in the art. When the *Poetics* is read in connection with such related treatises as the *Rhetoric* and the *Politics,* it is seen in its practical aspect as a handbook for poets, just as the *Rhetoric* is a manual for orators and the *Politics* a guidebook for statesmen. In this respect it resembles Horace's *Epistle to the Pisos,* the *Ars poetica,* but unlike Horace's treatise, the *Poetics* is neither peremptory nor cynical in tone. It is a serious and diligent inquiry organized around a basic axiom, and while it probably would be of little practical help to a budding poet, it would certainly serve to orient him in the fundamentals of the art.

The aim of tragedy, it is assumed, is the purgation of fear and pity. In order to be purged, these emotions must first be aroused and mobilized. Tragedy is specifically designed for this purpose. The tragic poem is not merely pleasurable. It is therapeutic.

This idea is not echoed elsewhere in the critical literature of antiquity. Tragedy was generally considered to be didactic: poets were teachers; poems taught lessons. For the Renaissance humanists, who had long brooded over the precepts of Horace and the tragedies of Seneca, the Aristotelian theory of catharsis was a revolutionary idea, It was widely quoted and interpreted, without being in the least understood. In other respects the *Poetics* made sense, and its elaboration led to a system of rules which had little relation to the works of the great Greek playwrights but was generally assumed to have the authority of Scripture. The three unities which were derived from the *Poetics* led to the development of a new dramatic genre which bore little resemblance to the ancient drama. At its best the new classicism resulted in a handful of authentic masterpieces. At its worst it was distinguished by a series of tedious tragedies whose redeeming feature was their correctness.

The *Poetics* touches very briefly on the origin of tragedy. In the fourth chapter of the *Poetics* it is said that tragedy began as an improvisation in the performance of the dithyramb. The dithyramb in honor of Dionysus was performed by a male choir which circled the altar of the god, singing his praises. At some point in its development, so we are told, the leader of the chorus varied the performance by improvising a dialogue with one of the choristers, thus introducing a dramatic element in what was basically a musical form. In time this combination acquired magnitude and style, and the meter of the dialogue was changed so that it came closer to the rhythms of colloquial speech. Aeschylus added a second actor and subordinated the choral element to the spoken parts of the play. Sophocles added a third actor. In this manner, according to the *Poetics,* tragedy developed its own natural form. It is possible that tragedy originated in this manner.[3] What can be said with confidence is that the origin of tragedy is uncertain.

The *Poetics* defines tragedy with admirable precision:

> A tragedy is the imitation of an action that is serious and complete, and of appropriate magnitude, in richly ornamented language of various kinds, each brought in separately in its proper place. It is represented by actors, not narrated, and includes incidents that arouse pity and fear so as to bring about a purgation of these emotions. By richly ornamented language I mean language that has rhythm, harmony and song, and by each kind separately I mean that some parts are in meter and some are sung.[4]

This definition distinguishes tragedy from comedy with respect to the seriousness of the subject and from other narrative poetry, such as the epic, which is not acted. The elements of tragedy are then enumerated in the order of their importance. There are six: plot, character, diction, thought, spectacle, and melody. Of these, plot and character are considered at length, and diction is gone into methodically. Thought, spectacle and melody are treated as accessories, not related essentially to the art of poetry:

> . . . melody is the most important of the pleasurable accessories of tragedy. The spectacle, though an attraction, requires less technical skill than the other parts, and has least to do with the art of poetry. The tragic effect may be achieved without performance and without actors and, besides, the devising of the spectacle concerns the scene-designer rather than the poet.[5]

Elsewhere, however, Aristotle concedes that the style of the production has a certain importance. Tragedy, he notes, is superior to epic poetry

> . . . since it has everything that epic poetry has, for it can even use the same meter, and also it has, as no trifling addition, the music and the spectacle which make the pleasure of tragedy more vivid, and this can be felt whether it is read or acted.[6]

Since the *Poetics* has to do primarily with poetry, it is understandable that Aristotle concerns himself little, if at all, with the staging, choreography or scenic display of drama. Consequently, aside from some hints in the plays of Aristophanes and some sculptures and paintings, we have little idea of the manner of production or the visual effects called for in the plays. Aristotle does not advise the poet to rely on the production for the effects he has in mind. The tragic effect is inherent in the drama, not in its representation:

> Fear and pity may be aroused by the spectacle, but they are better aroused by the structure and incidents of the play, and this shows the better poet. The plot should be so ordered that, even without seeing the play, anyone who hears the account of what happened is thrilled with horror and pity. It is so when one is told the story of Oedipus. To produce this same effect by visual means is less artistic and requires extraneous assistance. Those who use such means to produce effects that are not fearful but merely monstrous have nothing in common with tragedy. Not every kind of pleasure should be looked for in tragedy, but only its own proper pleasure.[7]
> Of the six parts of tragedy enumerated in the *Poetics,* the most important is, we are told, the plot:

Since in tragedy the representation is performed by living actors, it follows necessarily that an essential part of the imitation is what is seen by the eye, and after that come melody and diction, for it is through these that they produce the imitation. By diction I mean here the metrical arrangement of the words, and by melody I mean all that commonly pertains to that term. And since the subject of imitation is an action performed by personages who of necessity have certain qualities of character and thought—for it is these which determine their success or failure—it follows that what represents the action is the plot. And by plot I mean here the arrangement of the happenings. Character defines the quality of the agents, and thought is expressed in those passages in which they make an argument or deliver an opinion.[8]

From the viewpoint of the *Poetics* the arrangement of the incidents *(ten synthesin ton pragmaton)* is the principal business of the poet in composing a tragedy. Since the shaping principle of the tragic action is its effectiveness in arousing fear and pity, it is the proper design of the plot *(mythos, logos)* that determines the success of the play, not the portrayal of the characters involved in it. On this point the *Poetics* is emphatic:

[Of the six elements of tragedy] the most important is the management of the incidents. Tragedy is an imitation not of men, but of actions and life, of happiness and misery. . . . Character gives men qualities, but it is their actions—what they do—that brings them happiness or misery. Accordingly, in a play they do not act in order to display their character. It is in the course of their actions that they show what they are. So that it is the action, the story or plot, that is the end and pur-

pose of a tragedy. . . . The essential thing, the ruling
principle and, so to speak, the soul of a tragedy is the
plot. . . .[9]

The incidents that are represented must be arranged, we
are told, so that they follow one another logically, without the
interpolation of extraneous matters:

> Of simple plots and actions, the episodic is the worst.
> I call a plot episodic when there is neither necessity nor
> probability in the sequence of events. Bad poets con-
> struct such plots because they know no better, and
> good poets in order to please the audience, for, since
> poets engage in contests, they are sometimes forced to
> stretch out a story beyond its capacity. . . . Tragedy is
> the imitation of an action that is both complete and
> inclusive of incidents that arouse pity and fear. Such
> incidents have the greatest effect when they occur
> unexpectedly and yet in consequence of one another.
> In such cases they are more astonishing than if they
> happen spontaneously or merely by chance. . . .[10]

The principle of logical sequence which is here enunciated
served the poets of the Renaissance admirably as a guide to
dramatic construction, but the type of tragedy which pleased
the audiences in the playhouses of the time of Shakespeare
necessarily made greater concessions to popular taste than anything designed for the theater of Dionysus. A consequence was
the genre of tragedy associated with the Elizabethan theater,
which gave scholars offence by mixing hornpipes with funerals.
In the French regular drama Aristotle's admonition, together
with his definition of tragedy, resulted in the principle of the
séparation des genres and strictly excluded comic scenes from
tragic plays. In time the mechanical application of Aristotle's

precept led to the development of the well-made play, which was so ingeniously and logically constructed that it was hardly true to life.

The *système du théâtre* developed under the influence of the *Poetics,* first by Pierre Corneille and afterwards by Augustin Scribe and Victorien Sardou, worked very well so long as the world of the theater had only an ideal relation to the outer world, but with the advent of realism in the drama, the artificiality of the Aristotelian idea of theater became increasingly apparent. In the time of Zola it became evident that "Life as it is" is patently irrational and episodic to a degree that would not be tolerated in a well-ordered play. It is clear that this fact was evident also to Aristotle. According to the *Poetics:*

> It is apparent from what has been said that it is not the business of the poet to tell what actually happened, but what might have happened in accordance with necessity and probability. Hence poetry is more philosophic and more serious than history, for poetry deals with things from a universal viewpoint, but history with particular things.[11]

Aristotle evidently believed that the universal had more reality than the particular and that the poet's business was to rearrange experience in conformity with logic and reason. The application of Aristotelian principles to the drama of later ages thus resulted in a theatrical system that was entirely plausible but not readily credible. This system was well adapted to the requirements of the Age of Reason, but it did not survive the intellectual ravages of the twentieth century.

It was, it would seem, from a passage of the *Poetics* that Antonin Artaud derived the idea of the Theater of Cruelty. In *Le Théâtre et son double,* he writes:

An idea of the theatre has been lost. At this stage of the decay of our sensibility it is clear that above all we need a theatre that will awaken us, heart and nerves. In these distressing and catastrophic times we urgently feel the need of a theatre which is not dwarfed by events, which will find resonance deep within us and dominate the instability of the times.

Long accustomed to diverting spectacles, we have forgotten the idea of a serious drama which, brushing aside the current shows, will inspire us with the burning magnetism of its images and will act therapeutically on our souls as an expression of unforgettable power.[12]

But Aristotle does not seem to have thought of tragedy as an assault on the nerves or a way of opening the primitive sources of the soul's vitality. In Aristotle's view tragedy affords an experience in the theater which, by discharging psychic tensions, restores inner peace. Tragedy, according to the *Poetics,* is a thrilling experience which arouses pain at the same time that it affords relief. The assumption is that the pressure of the suppressed fears and anxieties that normally afflict the soul will be pumped up in the theater and discharged in a painful but harmless emotional outburst and that after this ordeal, the spectator will go about his business calmly, all passion spent.

In the *Poetics* Aristotle does not specifically discuss the nature of the emotions that tragedy is designed to arouse. There is, however, some discussion of their nature in the *Rhetoric.* This essay is more closely concerned than the *Poetics* with the nature of audiences and the ways in which an assembly may be moved through the skill of the speaker. Among other oratorical skills, Aristotle considers the methods for mobilizing and directing such emotions as shame, indignation, pity and fear.

The methods are those of the dramatist. The emotions are given a useful definition:

> Pity may be defined as a feeling of pain caused by the sight of some evil, destructive or hurtful, which befalls one who does not deserve it, and which we might expect to befall ourselves or our friends, and moreover, to befall us soon.[13]

It would appear from this definition that Aristotle's idea of pity does not carry the sense of compassion, the generous outgoing feeling of sympathy that we normally associate with this term. Pity, as Aristotle defines it, is a species of anxiety, analogous to fear, aroused by the undeserved misfortune of another, which we may expect shortly to share. In identifying sympathetically with another's misery we are really fearing for ourselves. Thus pity and fear are closely related perturbations, both self-centered:

> Fear may be defined as a pain or disturbance due to a mental image of some destructive or painful evil in the future. I mean only such evils as amount to great pain or loss. And even these only if they appear not remote, but so near as to seem imminent: we do not fear things that are a long way off. Consequently, when it is advisable that the audience should be frightened, the orator must make them feel that they are really in danger of something, pointing out that it has happened to others who were stronger than they.[14]

In Aristotle's estimation, evidently, the art of tragedy has close relations with the art of oratory. The personages depicted in tragedy are, in some sense, orators, and since they use the rhetorical arts to gain their ends, it is the business of the dramatist to make them express such thoughts as will best further their purpose. It is also the dramatist's business to arouse in his audience an appropriate emotional response with regard to the behavior of his personages. It follows that the poet and the orator pursue similar courses, though with different aims. The tragic poet seeks to frighten his audience for therapeutic reasons; the orator, in order to direct its actions. But while the orator normally deals with human relations, the poet is concerned with the relations of man and god. The world of Tragedy is not the practical world of everyday experience. It is a dream world, the domain of myth, in which pity is a feeling of human kinship and fear is indistinguishable from awe.

THE PLOT

The tragic plot is designed for effect, and to be properly effective the action represented must be of appropriate magnitude. The *Poetics* suggests a simple precept:

> An action must be of such length as can be readily accommodated in the memory.[15]

As for the duration of the incidents represented on the stage, however, the suggestion is more precise. Epic poetry, we are told:

> . . . is unlimited in time, while tragedy tends to fall within a single circuit of the sun, or something near it.[16]

Although this observation would seem to summarize dramatic practice in the fifth century, in fact the Greek tragedies with which we are familiar do not conform with it. Nevertheless it resulted in the iron-clad rule which in the Renaissance became the mark of classic tragedy. The forms of Greek tragedy were transmitted to Rome in terms that suggest that rigor mortis had long ago set in, but Horace says nothing special with regard to the duration of the action in tragedy. Horace was certainly aware that the vividness of a play would be in some relation to the unity of its action:

> Be your subject what it will, only let it be simple and one.[17]

The good poet

> ... does not date "The Return of Diomed" from Meleager's death, nor the Trojan war from the egg; he hastens to the crisis, and carries the auditor into the midst of things as though the story was already known; what he despairs of clarifying, he omits, and so employs fiction, so blends false with true, that beginning, middle and end all strike the same chord.[18]

The *Ars poetica* is, no doubt, the work of a master poet, but Horace did not write plays and was not especially familiar with the theater. His treatise is a collection of stereotypes rather haphazardly strung together. Its ultimate source may well have been the *Poetics,* but Horace appears to have relied more directly on a Greek work on the art of poetry by Neoptolemus of Parium. At any rate, though its influence on the literature of the Renaissance surpassed the influence of Aristotle, the *Ars poetica* was not the source of the unities of time and place.

The result of the classical precepts with regard to the proper way to tell a story in the theater, together with the Senecan examples, was a series of tragic plays which placed the point of attack immediately before the denouement. This made for a remarkably concise dramatic narrative which excluded action and necessitated extensive exposition. In these circumstances French regular tragedy acquired a lyrical and elegiac quality which was very far from the scheme advocated in the *Poetics.*

In the *Poetics* the so-called unity of time is not the subject of extensive discussion. It seems clear that the restriction of the action to the events of a single day had more to do, in Aristotle's estimation, with the concentration of the action than with doubts regarding the ability of the audience to accord the passage of time on the stage with the passage of time in the auditorium. Aristotle nowhere requires the imitation of action to be exact, nor did the Greek poets have any such idea. It was the sixteenth-century humanists who invented the unities.

The *Agamemnon* takes place over an indefinite period of time. The beacon on the mountaintop is sighted, presumably, some little time after the sack of Troy, but it would take many days for Agamemnon's ship to cross the Aegean, and apparently nobody saw any inconvenience in having this interval covered by a choral song in a matter of minutes. In the *Eumenides,* similarly, the long interval between the scene in Delphi and the trial in Athens is covered by a single stasimon. In the Greek theater, it appears, no one was concerned with the ability of the audience to imagine the passage of weeks or perhaps years in the space of some minutes. The Renaissance critics, however, were extremely solicitous in this regard.

The rules with which they saddled the poets of their time were usually justified on the basis of verisimilitude. It was therefore prescribed that ideally the time of representation should correspond exactly with the time required for the action represented to take place. In his version of the *Poetics* the sixteenth-century critic Lodovico Castelvetro wrote:

> It is not possible to make an audience suppose that several days and nights have passed when they have the evidence of their senses that only a few hours have gone by.[19]

Consequently, he concludes:

> Tragedy cannot represent any action except such as occurs in one place and within the space of twelve hours. . . .[20]

The restriction was generally accepted. It was not generally welcomed. A century after Castelvetro's *Poetica* Pierre Corneille described the playwright's struggle with the unities:

> It is necessary to observe unity of action, place and time. That nobody doubts. But there is no small difficulty in knowing what unity of action is, or how far one can extend these unities of time and place.

Of the unity of time, he wrote:

> Many object to this rule, which they call tyrannical, and they would be right if it was founded solely on the authority of Aristotle. But what makes it acceptable is the natural reason that supports it. The dramatic poem is an imitation or, better said, a portrait of the actions of men, and it is beyond doubt that the best portraits are those that come closest to the original. A performance lasts two hours, and it would be a perfect likeness if the action it represented took no longer for its realization. Thus, let us not worry about whether it is 12 or 24 hours, but let us compress the action of the poem within the least possible duration, so that the representation should resemble it best and most perfectly. . . .[21]

In the next generation Racine took this idea somewhat further. The need to observe the unities, he felt, led the poet to an elegant simplicity of plot:

In tragedy it is only the verisimilar that is effective. And what verisimilitude is there when in one day there happens a multitude of things that could hardly take place in several weeks? There are those who think that simplicity implies a lack of invention. They do not realize that, on the contrary, invention really consists in making something out of nothing, and that multiplicity of incident has always been the refuge of poets who had neither the abundance nor the strength to hold the attention of their spectators through five acts by means of a single action, sustained by the violence of the passions, the beauty of the sentiments, and the elegance of the expression.[22]

Nothing is said in the *Poetics* with regard to the unity of place. Greek theater in the fifth century was not well adapted, obviously, to facilitate frequent changes of scene, but it is likely that by the time of Sophocles painted screens were used to orient the setting, and there is evidence that the periaktoi served to indicate a change of scene. The existing tragedies do not, in fact, call for a multiplicity of scenes, but while scene changes are infrequent, there appears to have been no difficulty in shifting the action from place to place when that was necessary. There are, for example, radical scene changes in the *Eumenides* and in the *Ajax,* and scenic effects indicated in other plays would tax the ingenuity of a modern scenic artist.

Tragedy, in the Renaissance, made no more pretense of realism than had tragedy in the Greek theater, yet Renaissance critics seem to have been obsessed with the need for verisimilitude. In regular tragedy the necessary effect was achieved not by extending the capabilities of the stage, but by limiting the scope of the action. The popular theater, on the other hand, reveled in multiplicity of scene and incident, although much, if not everything, was left to the imagination of the audience. Shakespeare's plots, like those of Lope de Vega, moved fluidly through space and time without inconveniencing the stage crew in the least, but those who tried to write tragedy in the manner of the ancients were content to shape their plots to suit the limitations of the conventional palace hall. This arrangement called for ingenuity and also made it possible to play a tragedy in a very restricted area at minimal expense, but it had the disadvantage of restricting the movement of the action to the point where a play became a series of declamations. When, with the production of *Le Cid*, Corneille at last opened a window on the closeness of French regular tragedy, he found it necessary to apologize for extending the unity of place beyond the permissible limits. He had found, he wrote,

> . . . no precept concerning it either in Aristotle or in Horace. This has led some to think that the rule was established only in consequence of the unity of time, and to extend it so as to admit any place to which a man can go and return within 24 hours. I believe, however, that we must try to make the unity as exact as possible, but as it does not suit every subject I should willingly grant that everything that takes place in the same city possesses unity of place.[23]

Racine, however, was not disposed to quibble with the unities. He accepted the rules without question—one might say, with enthusiasm. The result is that his tragedies are miracles of fine workmanship, a string of exquisite cameos, precious in themselves, and completely alien to the spirit of the *Poetics*.

One may well wonder why dramatists of this stature were willing to accept restrictions that had no real basic in antiquity. The explanation, perhaps, has something to do with the protocol of the courtly audience they served, but it is likely that the unities were accepted, as I have suggested, in the same spirit that prompted the Greek poets to accept the cast-restrictions of the Greek theater. The seventeenth-century French poets were in the highest sense craftsmen, and the rigidity of the system within which they worked enormously enhanced the difficulty of their art. Within the straitened limits of the unities they developed a style of classic drama which was highly sucessful and in its way superb, but widely distant from the practice of the classic poets.

In the *Poetics* the unity of action is defined in terms of the relation of a whole to its parts:

> Now a whole is that which has a beginning, a middle and an end. A beginning is something that does not necessarily follow something else, but naturally implies something coming after it. An end is that which naturally follows something as its necessary or usual consequence, but is not necessarily followed by anything more. A middle is that which naturally comes after something and is necessarily followed by something else. A well-constructed plot, therefore, cannot begin or end wherever one likes. Its beginning and end must be related in the manner described.[24]

This formulation involves the principle of logical sequence which the *Poetics* everywhere affirms as essential to a well-ordered plot. Moreover, a series of incidents firmly linked in the order of cause and consequence would not only have unity, but would reject the inclusion of extraneous incidents:

> A plot is not unified, as some think, because it is concerned with one man, for many things happen to a man, some of which cannot be combined in a single unit. . . . The truth is that, just as in the other mimetic

arts it is one thing only that is imitated, so in poetry the plot, as an imitation of an action, should imitate one action only, as a complete whole, with its parts so clearly arranged that if any one part is moved or omitted the whole is disarranged and disjointed, for what makes no perceptible difference by its presence or absence is no real part of the whole.[25]

A strict application of this precept would result in an ideal narrative structure of which it is rare to find a successful example in the tragic or epic poetry of the Greeks—or, indeed, anywhere else. As it was ultimately formulated in such influential works as Tasso's *Discorsi* of 1594 or Lope de Vega's *Arte nuevo de hacer comedias* of 1609, it set up a salutary principle of composition which was everywhere quoted with reverence and everywhere violated.[26]

In Greek tragedies the point of attack is usually set so late that there is little room for a multiplicity of incidents. But the Greek poets do not seem to have been overly concerned with the question of unity. Few of the existing tragedies have the tight structure that Aristotle admired in the *Oedipus Tyrannus.* Most of them were composed in accordance with looser ideas of playmaking. The *Eumenides,* for example, has a double outcome: there is no compelling need to convert the Furies after the acquittal of Orestes; the two ends of the play are connected largely by a happy association of ideas. *Antigone* also ends twice: the tragic emphasis falls first on Antigone, afterwards on Creon. *Hippolytus* develops a plot within a plot: it is obviously unnecessary to involve the squabble of celestial powers in the unfortunate passion of Phaedra for Hippolytus. *The Trojan Women* is a collocation of pathetic episodes which, however touching, falls short of a plot and has no terminal principle. These plays, while they lack unity of action, are nevertheless marvelously effective drama. The question of whether they would be more effective if more closely knit seems frivolous.

But if the unity of action had not much basis in the actual practice of those who wrote for the Periclean theater, it had everything to do with Aristotle's idea of the aim of tragedy. The Renaissance critics were inclined to the view that the purpose of tragedy was primarily didactic, and therefore they condoned the inclusion of sermonic passages and admonitory speeches which detracted from the unity of the action. The Aristotelian principle of unity, though everywhere quoted with respect, had no special influence on the tragedies of those who wrote for the popular stage in England, and the Spanish dramatists declined to be bound by it. But in Italy, and more particularly in France, the principle of unity subjected the writers of regular tragedy to a galling discipline. Corneille had trouble in justifying the amours of the Infanta and Don Sanche in *Le Cid.* The inclusion of Aricie in *Phèdre* was easier to justify, but was nevertheless unnecessary from the standpoint of the *Poetics.* The Renaissance playwrights did not question the authority of Aristotle, but their plays were not designed to purge the audience of its fears, and they had no need to concentrate the action for that purpose. For the Renaissance poet, unity was not an exigency of the plot. It was a matter of elegance, the mark of good craftsmanship, and a proper respect for authority.

DESIGN

The Greek poets did not, as a rule, invent the stories they dramatized. Their material was legendary. It was therefore the manner in which the old stories were presented that showed the skill and originality of the poet. In these circumstances, characterization gave more scope to the dramatist's talents than did narrative. In the *Poetics* the preeminence of the plot as the essential element of tragedy is stressed with such vehemence as to suggest that already in its day character portrayal was being emphasized at the expense of plot. But in Aristotle's opinion it was not through the portrayal of character that fear and pity were aroused, but through the impact of the action.

The *Poetics* treats the design of the plot at some length and from several points of view. There are, we are told, two parts to every plot:

> In every tragedy there is the tying and the loosing. What happens before the opening scene, and some of the following incidents, constitutes the tying; the rest is the loosing. By the tying I mean all the story up to the point where the hero's fortunes change; by the loosing all from the beginning of the change to the end.[27]

The metaphor in this passage is not altogether happy, nor is the image altogether clear. In English we have no word for this "tying": we come closest with *complication.* As for "loosing," we are forced to use the French *dénouement,* which is no less mysterious. The figure seems to refer to spinning; a plot is pictured as a yarn rather than a texture. In Aristophanes's comedy, Lysistrata explains:

> When we are winding thread and it tangles, we pass the spool across and through the skein, now this way, now that, until it is free.[28]

This does not go very far to describe the design of a tragedy. Earlier in the *Poetics,* however, tragedy is likened to an organism, something that has a beginning, middle and end. This suggests a tripartite structure (exposition, complication, and resolution), while the later passage implies a dual structure (a pests or trochees. The kommos is a lamentation sung by the chorus and actor in concert.[30]

The *Poetics* analyzes the design of the plot also from a thematic standpoint. Here two common narrative devices are introduced:

> Plots are either simple or complex, since the actions they imitate can be of either sort. When the action proceeds continuously from beginning to end, I call it simple if the change of fortune takes place without peripety [peripeteia] or recognition [anagnorisis]. I call it complex when the change involves either of these or both. These should result from the arrangement of the plot, as inevitable or probable consequences of what has gone before. . . .[31]

This passage distinguishes a plot that sets forth a linear chain of events from one which is turned by an unexpected happening or disclosure. A reversal (peripeteia) is said to be a change of the hero's fortunes to their opposite, but apparently the word is meant to indicate something more than the reversal which is the common characteristic of tragic plots. The example in the *Poetics* is taken from the *Oedipus:*

> . . . here the opposite state of things is produced by the man who, meaning to gladden Oedipus and to allay his fears regarding his mother, reveals instead the secret of his birth.[32]

The implication is that a peripety occurs when an action brings about a consequence contrary to what is expected. It is not clear whether the term refers to a special kind of reversal or to a reversal in general, a metabasis.

tangling and a straightening out). Practically there is not much difference between these two patterns; neither is particularly apt. The formula transmitted by Donatus with regard to comedy was found equally acceptable in describing the design of tragedy:

> Every comedy is divided into four parts, the Prologue, the Protasis, the Epitasis and the Catastrophe. . . . The first part, or Protasis, is the beginning of the dramatic action. In it, part of the play is revealed and part withheld in order to create suspense. The second part, or Epitasis, marks the further development of difficulties and is, as I have said, the knot [*nodus*] of the entire coil. The last part, or Catastrophe, is the solution, pleasing to the audience, and made clear to all by an explanation of what has passed.[29]

This time-honored formula incorporates the analogy of the tying and loosing of a knot which we find in the *Poetics*. It describes the structure of Terentian comedy quite well but sheds little light on the shape of a Greek tragic plot. The formal design of Greek tragedy is of quite another order. The description of this design in the *Poetics* is quite precise, though the passage seems to be an interpolation and is in any case clumsy:

> From the point of view of its separate sections, a tragedy has the following parts: prologue, episode, exode, and a choral portion, parodos and stasimon. These two are common to all tragedies, whereas songs from the stage and kommoi are found in some. The prologue is all that precedes the parodos of the chorus. An episode is all that comes between the two choral songs. The exodos is all that follows the last choral song. In the choral part the parodos is the whole first statement of the chorus. A stasimon is a choral song without ana-

In Aristotle's opinion the reversal of fortune—peripety or metabasis—should bring about a change from happiness to misery in the hero's fortunes in order to make the effect proper to tragedy:

> . . . the change in the hero's fortunes must be not from misery to happiness, but from happiness to misery. . . . Critics who blame Euripides for following this course in his tragedies by giving them an unhappy ending are wrong. It is, as I have said, the proper course to take.[33]

Evidently the happy ending, though it did not meet with Aristotle's approval, was consonant with his idea of the aim of tragedy as a means of eliciting fear and pity. It is certainly possible to design a tragic plot so that the emotional crisis occurs at some point prior to the reversal that brings about a happy outcome. *Iphigenia in Tauris, Ion, Helen,* and *Alcestis* are effective tragedies that end happily, and everything indicates that they were well received. Aristotle does not express admiration for the type of plot in which the good are made happy and the wicked are punished. That sort of play, we are told,

> . . . ranks first only through the weakness of the audience; the poets merely follow the wishes of their public. But the pleasure here is not the pleasure of tragedy. It belongs rather to comedy. . . .[34]

In Aristotle's view the pleasure of tragedy is akin to pain. Tragedy requires neither the relief of a happy outcome, nor the sugar-coating of poetic justice, nor any justification beyond the pleasure it affords. As Aristotle sees it, tragedy is a potent alcohol. Its savor is sharp.

A frequent device in plotting a reversal of fortune is a sudden revelation of identity. In the *Poetics,* anagnorisis—usually translated in English as "discovery" or "recognition"—is given a clear definition:

> Discovery, as the word indicates, is a change from ignorance to knowledge that results in a reversal of disposition on the part of those marked out for good or evil fortune. The most effective form of discovery is that which brings about a reversal, such as that which takes place in the *Oedipus.* . . . A discovery of that sort followed by a peripety will arouse either pity or fear, and it is actions such as these that, according to our hypothesis, tragedy imitates.[35]

Four types of discovery are enumerated in the *Poetics:* discovery by tokens, by self-revelation, by some inadvertent act, and by inference. Discovery—or recognition—by tokens is a very frequent device. In the *Choephoroi* Electra recognizes her brother by the tunic she once made for him; apparently he is still wearing it. In Euripides's *Electra* he is recognized, more plausibly, by a scar on his forehead. Ion is recognized, in Euripides's play, by the tokens with which he was exposed as an infant. But Oedipus is recognized by inference.

In the type of plot characteristic of modern drama the manipulation of a reversal through a discovery is still a useful narrative device, but in the modern theater, with its emphasis on character, recognitions are more often psychological than revelations of kinship. Many of Shaw's comedies, for instance, turn upon an anagnorisis. In *Androcles and the Lion* Lavinia tells the ultrapacifist Ferrovius that he will discover his true self in his hour of trial, and in the Roman arena Ferrovius indeed discovers what he is. In plots of this sort the playwright's task is to devise hours of trial in which his characters may discover themselves, and the recognition is the shaping principle of the plot.

In Greek tragedy the revelation is seldom characterological. The reversal generally turns upon a discovery of kinship. In the *Iphigenia in Tauris* and in Euripides's *Helen* the recognition is simple and decisive. In the *Oedipus Tyrannus* it comprises the whole of the action. But in none of these plays is the recognition other than a question of social relationships. It is not until the age of Shakespeare that the portrayal of character becomes of vital concern to the dramatist, and it was neither Sophocles nor Aristotle who influenced the age in that respect. It was Seneca.

MOTIVATION

In discussing the type of plot that is most suitable for tragedy, Aristotle, as we have seen, disparages the idea of a double outcome, in accordance with poetic justice. The tragic effect, in his opinion, is not designed to satisfy our sense of the rightness of things, but to arouse our sense of the perilous nature of the human situation. From this standpoint, tragedy is a manifestation of the retribution of the gods and the disadvantages of provoking their displeasure. Indeed, *Prometheus Bound* depicts Zeus as a tyrant who would have utterly destroyed mankind had not the titan taught man the arts of survival. The figure quite aptly describes man's unending struggle with nature, and so far as mankind is concerned, it is not reassuring. The tragic effect, in Aristotle's view, is not designed to be comfortable.

In the *Poetics* Aristotle is concerned, not with the problem of evil, but with the instruction of poets. In order to achieve the tragic effect and the consequent catharsis, the tragic hero must be such as to induce the audience to identify with his suffering.

Since he is to arouse pity, he cannot be depicted as a wicked man, for the sufferings of the wicked elicit not pity, but satisfaction. On the other hand, we are told:

> ... it is not advisable to show good men passing from happiness to misery for that arouses neither fear nor pity, but is simply shocking. ... There remains then, the mean between these two. This is the man who is not pre-eminently virtuous and just, whose misfortune is due to no badness or depravity, but to some error [*hamartia*] such as might be made by men of high station and good fortune such as Oedipus and Thyestes and famous men of similar extraction.[36]

The proximate cause of misfortune is thus, according to the *Poetics,* an error. The Greek word *hamartia* was associated with archery and referred to a bad shot, a shot that missed the mark—by extension, an offense. It does not appear to denote a characterological defect. The idea that the fall of the tragic hero is the result of a flaw of character is certainly consonant with the scheme of character analysis developed in Aristotle's *Nichomachean Ethics* and in the *Characters* of Theophrastus, and it gained a firm foothold in Renaissance psychology. But tragedy, in Aristotle's view, is concerned primarily with action, not character. For the purpose of the tragic poem there is no need to characterize the hero as someone genetically inclined to make mistakes. To bring about misfortune a single error will suffice. It is unnecessary for the tragic hero to make a habit of error.

Since it is hardly possible to define Aristotle's idea of a hamartia, the subject has been one of much controversy. The notion that the hero invites disaster by reason of what he is, rather than what he does, finds some support in such plays as the *Oedipus Tyrannus* and the *Ajax.* But Oedipus's error is not due to a flaw of character: what is at fault is his lineage; he was doomed before he was born.

Oedipus is indeed characterized as an unduly irascible man, but it is fate that destroys him, not his bad temper. Among the heroes of tragedy, Sophocles's Ajax and his Creon in the *Antigone* and Euripides's Jason in the *Medea* and his Hippolytus display traits that predispose them to commit tragic errors, but the notion that the hero's misfortune is the result of a specific characterological defect is not useful in rationalizing the Greek sense of the tragic. Nor, it must be admitted, is the tragic mood greatly clarified by the idea that the hero's downfall is the result of an honest error of judgment. The Greek sense of the tragic is rooted far too deeply for such simple explanations, and the author of the *Poetics* very wisely avoids the question.

The personages of Greek tragedy are never portrayed as wholly ingratiating figures. The tragic kings are stock types, haughty, hot-tempered, suspicious and vindictive, the human prototypes of the Olympian deities. They are good men but not lovable. In the *Poetics* Aristotle recommends a plot which elicits fear and pity without arousing indignation. Consequently the downfall of the tragic hero must be in some way justified. In the *Prometheus* the titan arouses sympathy; but he is obviously a nuisance in the cosmic administration. The chorus in the plays of Aeschylus and Sophocles is concerned to reassure the audience with regard to the workings of divine justice, though the action seldom does much to bear it out. The gods are, no doubt, just. They can be depended on. But they are not friendly gods, and their justice does not arouse enthusiasm.

In the *Oedipus Tyrannus* Jocasta tries to calm her husband's fears by telling him that there is no such thing as fate:

> Why should men feel fear when all depends on chance,
> and nothing that is to come can be predicted? It is best

to live with a light heart as long as one can, without troubling one's head about the future.[37]

But as the play elaborately demonstrates, it is not chance but destiny that rules the world. Everything is predictable. In the case of Oedipus the prophecy is fully justified by the event, and though Laius and, after him, Oedipus take every precaution to avert misfortune, all that was predicted comes to pass. Consequently, Oedipus accepts his fate without protest. His doom was written. The question of justice is not raised by any character in the play, and least of all by the chorus. Nevertheless the play is disquieting: the agony of Oedipus is patently undeserved, and his fate elicits not only pity, but indignation. Obviously the justice of the gods leaves something to be desired.

It is hardly possible, of course, to extend this attitude to Greek tragedy in general. But Euripides was evidently not satisfied with the dispositions of heaven, and in the plays both of Aeschylus and Sophocles there is perceptible a tinge of bitterness at the way in which the world is ordered: great drama is always in opposition. Sophocles was reputedly a member of the upper class and politically a staunch conservative. It is likely that in the time of the *Oedipus Tyrannus* the Delphic oracle was under fire for partisanship. In the *Tyrannus* the chorus calls upon Zeus to substantiate the oracles of Apollo in the interests of religion. Since Oedipus has done everything to save the city, the invocation seems hardly in character:

> I will go no more to pray at the holy place at the navel of the world, nor to Abae or Olympia, unless the oracles are proven true for all men's hands to point to. O Zeus, if you are rightly called king of the world, do not let this occasion slip from your immortal grasp. The oracles

regarding Laius are old now and faded, and no one pays attention to them. Apollo is no longer honored. God's worship perishes.[38]

As it turns out, Zeus does his duty by the oracle, and Apollo's honor is saved. It is saved, of course, at the expense of Oedipus, who is guilty only of being the son of Laius. Laius has already paid for his sins, but the account is not closed. Those who inherit the blood of the culpable inherit also the curse that taints it. The sin of Oedipus is original sin, for which God exacts due payment. To a modern reader the irony of the situation is painfully apparent. How it seemed to the audience for which it was originally intended is impossible to say. It was many years after he presented the *Tyrannus* that Sophocles thought to redress the balance. In the *Oedipus Coloneus* Oedipus is brought to Colonus to die a mysterious death in the service of forces which in some sense sanctify him. Evidently, in Sophocles's view, the gods are just in their dealings with humanity, They are, however, merciless. Zeus rules the world. But he does not love it; and in this unhappy thought is rooted the sense of the tragic.

In the type of plot that turns on an error, the Greek poets found it interesting to demonstrate the irony of fate by offering the tragic hero a choice of two errors. Agamemnon, for instance, is trapped before ever he sets foot on the Trojan beach. His downfall, like his triumph, is predetermined, for he has inherited the sins of Atreus, and at the very outset of the Trojan enterprise he is hooked on the horns of a dilemma from which there is no escape: he must choose between the sacrifice of his daughter and the dispersal of his navy. In the *Iphigenia at Aulis* the wrath of Artemis is hardly clarified; what is clear is the fatal choice into which she drives Agamemnon, the choice which ultimately brings about his death. In the meantime his success is marked by a series of offenses so great that his apprehension at treading on the cloths at Mycenae actually borders on the comic.

In the world of tragedy a hero's life is a precarious adventure, and the admonition Know Thyself might well bear the meaning of Watch Your Step. In this world it is impossible to set afoot any considerable enterprise without the risk of offending some supernatural power. In such circumstances the tragic chorus is unanimous in counseling passivity, for at every crossroads the enterprising hero finds fatal errors awaiting him. Of these the most hazardous are those which attend success. The word for those is *hubris*.

Like many ancient words whose worth's unknown although their height be taken, the word *hubris* defies translation. The word is Homeric. It first occurs in the *Iliad*. In the tragedies it refers to the risk incurred by those who advance themselves in the world beyond permissible limits.

In the Christian mythology hubris is equated with pride, and is accounted a cardinal sin. But Greek hubris is not synonymous with pride. Its meaning is more usefully conveyed by such terms as insolence, arrogance, or excessive ambition. It is the mark of the dangerous subject, whose interests threaten those of his superiors: an undue assertion of the ego.

It is said of Thrasybulus of Miletus that, when his advice was sought on the subject of effective government, he took his client for a walk through a field of grain, lopping off with his stick the stalks that overtopped the others. In the world of mythology the gods appear to govern after some such system. In tragedy, when the gods are characterized, they are depicted usually as magnified images of an earthly tyrant. In Plato's *Republic* Socrates is made to express concern over the influence such ideas might have on the youth of a well-ordered state:

Mothers tell these lies to their children, saying that the gods prowl the streets at night in the likeness of strangers from distant lands. . . .[39]

Tragedy is such stuff as dreams are made on, and it is entirely consonant with the viewpoint of the *Poetics* that the tragic poets should make use of the myths that frighten children. In the *Agamemnon* the chorus recalls the sins on which rests the greatness of the house of Atreus. Prominent among these is its prosperity, which the gods cannot forgive. Riches, we are told, are seldom the fruit of virtue; for men amass wealth mainly at the expense of other men, and along with their gold they store up guilt:

> Goodness shines bright in the smoke of humble houses. She blesses the paths of the just. She turns away from the gilded palaces built by bloodstained hands and, heedless of gold, falsely stamped by flattery, she comes to dwell in the houses of the pure in heart.[40]

The suggestion is that the fall of Agamemnon was not the result of any special sin, although he was guilty of many. His offense was inherent in his success. To rise high is to risk a fall, for Zeus is envious: it is not for nothing that he is called *to phthoneros,* the jealous one. It is dangerous to come to his attention, and since the other gods are equally touchy, the hero's path is beset with pitfalls. It is prudent, therefore, to avoid any unusual display. In Aeschylean tragedy the chorus consistently disclaims any desire to rise above its station:

> There is proclaimed among mankind an ancient saying: man's prosperity does not die childless. When it has reached maturity it bears offspring: from man's good fortune springs endless misery for his children.[41]

The chorus concedes, however, that it is evil that breeds evil. The sins of the fathers are transmitted, but righteousness confers blessings on a prosperous house. Nonetheless the old men generally agree that it is best not to aim too high. In the *Oedipus Tyrannus* the chorus dwells on the dangers of civic ambition:

> Hubris breeds tyranny. When allied with wealth and power ambition gives rise to the pride that mounts the heights and is invariably overthrown. May the gods never end that contention that is good for the city. But as for that arrogance that fears not Dike nor respects the holy shrines, may it perish![42]

Hubris incurs nemesis: the gods cannot brook rivalry. This idea, everywhere implicit in Greek myth, is entirely explicit in the *History* of Herodotus, Sophocles's contemporary. The collision of human aspiration with the boundaries set by the divine powers is the shaping principle of the work. A familiar example is the story of Polycrates in the third book of the *History*. There we learn that the continual good fortune of Polycrates, the piratical tyrant of Samos, so disquieted Amasa, his Egyptian ally, that Amasa felt it necessary to advise his friend to ward off the envy of heaven by making an appropriate sacrifice. Accordingly, Polycrates cast into the sea the emerald signet that above all he valued. It was done in vain. The next day the ring was returned in the magnificent fish that was served up for his dinner. At this news King Amasa hastened to break off his alliance. Needless to say, Polycrates ultimately perished in a manner, writes Herodotus, that is not fit to be described.[43]

In Greek mythology, however, the gods are not altogether implacable, and in some cases their anger can be averted, we are told, by a timely sacrifice. Polycrates's sacrifice was unacceptable, but in the *Agamemnon* the chorus observes that though man is liable to sudden disaster, like a ship that strikes a hidden reef:

> Yet, if before this happens, with a measured cast, some precious portion of the cargo is consigned to the waves, not all of the vessel, though heavy with ruin, shall founder, nor the hull sink deep into the sea.[44]

Herodotus, however, takes a less optimistic view. In the *History* the sage Artabanus warns Xerxes that god will not tolerate excessive ambition:

> It is plain that he loves to bring down everything that exalts itself . . . for god permits nobody to have high thoughts but himself alone.[45]

Thus, in Greek tragedy the uneasy relation of man and god gives the hero constant cause for apprehension. Hubris is the occupational hazard of the great. As the world is constituted, the permissible limits of human aspiration are narrow; the hero's horizon, however, is wide, and in the conflict between the heroic ego and the jealous powers that hem it in, the Greek poets found the dynamic element which gives tragedy its grandeur as well as its sadness.

In this drama the gods are always busy and ever vigilant to defend their interests, but the grandeur of tragedy derives not only from the magnitude of the struggle, but from the knowledge that, though the gods control our lives, they do not live them. That is our portion: as mortals, we do not devise our destiny, but it is ours to fulfill it. It is man that plays the human drama. If there is applause, it is for him to take the bow.

The hero is born to suffer. He suffers because he is driven, for reasons he cannot know, to exert himself beyond human possibility, and at some point he is thwarted, inevitably, by agencies—perhaps inherent in himself—that cannot tolerate his greatness. It is at this point that his situation becomes tragic, and his behavior dramatically interesting.

The tragic hero suffers. His travail is obviously fruitless; it serves no purpose. When he has done his turn, the hero will be consigned, like lesser beings, to the scrap heap. The entire process is demonstrably pointless, a practical joke that nature plays upon itself, a jape at its own expense. But tragedy does not dwell on the absurd. It is not a celebration of death. It is an affirmation of life, and this is the source of its poetry. It goes without saying that this poetry magnificently sublimates the human neurosis.

CHARACTER

Since the *Poetics* is primarily concerned with the composition of a dramatic narrative, the discussion naturally centers on the plot. The portrayal of the characters involved in the drama is, in Aristotle's view, of secondary interest, necessary only insofar as it serves to justify the action. Beyond this point, characterization is largely cosmetic. The characters, nevertheless, must be properly presented:

Concerning character [*ethos*] there are four things to aim at. First of all, the characters must be good. Any type of person may be good, even a woman or a slave, though the one may be considered an inferior being, and the other beneath consideration. The second thing is to characterize them appropriately. A character may be manly; but it is not appropriate for a woman to be manly or clever. The third thing is that a personage should act in character, and this is different from being good or appropriate, in our sense of the term. The fourth is to make them consistent. . . .[46]

It is doubtful that precepts of this sort would be of much use to a modern playwright, but it must be remembered that Aristotle had in mind a theater far different from ours. Greek tragedy was a play of masks. Its characters served principally to move the plot and were necessarily much more abstract than the characters that populate the plays of the modern theater. In these circumstances such terms as "good," "bad," "manly," or "stupid" served rather to describe action than to delineate personality. Thus, in Chapter 13 of the *Poetics* we are told that the tragic protagonist should be neither vicious nor depraved, for the misfortunes of the wicked do not excite pity. Obviously Aristotle considered characterization to be largely functional; he evinces no interest in character as such. There are, in fact, no vicious characters in Greek tragedy. Such characters are first encountered in the plays of Seneca: it was from Seneca, not Sophocles, that Renaissance drama borrowed its villains. Though Greek tragedy has no lack of unpleasant characters like Jason or Aegisthus, none of these is portrayed as an evil person. Greek tragedy has no villains.

The principle which in the *Poetics* is called appropriateness *(harmonía)* is rendered in the *Ars poetica* of Horace by the Latin *decor.* Renaissance critics called this quality decorum and gave the principle a prominent place in their discussions of character. Giraldi wrote:

> The poet should pay heed to decorum, which is nothing other than what is fitting to places, times and persons. In short, decorum is nothing other than the grace or fitness of things, and should be considered not only in actions, but also in speeches and replies.[47]

The result of the principle of decorum was the shaping of dramatic characters in accordance with preconceived archetypes. In time this led to the formation of acting companies composed of line actors who specialized in playing stereotyped parts. Aristotle evidently saw no advantage in characterizing contrary to type, even though the Greek poets provided interesting examples of inappropriate characterization. Some of the memorable women of Greek tragedy—Clytemnestra, Medes, Alcestis, Hecuba—are inappropriately manly and clever, and characters like Jason and Admetus are inappropriately unmanly. For Aristotle, however, such deviants are useful only insofar as they serve the plot that involves them. From this viewpoint, it makes no difference in the story of Orestes whether Orestes is tall or short, witty or dull, nor does it matter whether Electra is pretty or plain. Thus, the touching scene of the nurse Cilissa in the *Choephoroi* is purely decorative. It serves no special purpose in furthering the action and is useful only insofar as it solicits the audience's pity for an abstract character who is in great need of sympathy, but can do without it. In a play written in strict conformity with Aristotelean principles it would be omitted.

The firm subordination of ethos to mythos in the *Poetics* suggests that the ancient audience did not require very much by way of characterization in order to animate the masks that moved about on the stage. In Greek tragedy, generally speaking, the tragic hero has a statuesque quality that is not altogether human. In the theater the tragic actor was remote from the audience, and it is clear that the Greek poet was at pains to distance tragic characters a long way from the marketplace. But it is clear also that, for Sophocles and Euripides at least, the temptation to peer behind the mask was occasionally irresistible. The Greek tragedies present us with an impressive gallery of dramatic portraits.

The *Oedipus Tyrannus* is memorable less because of the tragic web from which the hero strives to clear himself than because of the display of character which this process entails. As the knot tightens about him, the wise and benevolent king turns first into an irascible tyrant, then into a frightened child, and ultimately into the magnificent figure who has blinded himself to the world around him. As an example of dramatic portraiture it is difficult to find anything comparable in the history of the drama, and it is altogether unlikely that Sophocles developed so masterly a characterization purely in the service of his plot. It would seem, on the contrary, that what mainly interested him was the opportunity the plot gave him to depict the effect of the unfolding revelation of guilt on the soul of his hero. As a detective story the *Oedipus* leaves something to be desired. As a character study it is an incomparable achievement.

In Greek tragedy the hand of fate is everywhere manifest. But however reassuring such a view may be from the standpoint of religion, a rigidly determined world-order vastly diminishes the scale of the tragic hero. In a world strictly controlled by external powers, the tragedy of man is, at best, a puppet show, and the dramatic interest shifts from the moving character to the hand that pulls the strings. In drama so constituted the action necessarily becomes the poet's paramount considera-tion, and the mask amply suffices to define the character.

Very likely such was the basis of the reasoning in the *Poet-ics.* Unless the tension between the character and the power that moves him becomes dramatically significant, as it does in the *Oedipus* or the *Medea,* not much is gained by a detailed portrayal of the subject. Without free will, the tragic hero is inert, and the characterization serves mainly to color the action. The depiction of Electra in the *Choephoroi* was evidently de-signed to justify the murder of Clytemnestra. It does so; the murder of Clytemnestra is a source of satisfaction. In his version of the myth Sophocles makes Electra violent and savagely vin-dictive. As a result, Electra forfeits our sympathy, and the mur-der of Clytemnestra fills us with horror. But these characteriza-tions have no special significance in the action of the play. It is

Apollo who motivates the action, not Orestes, and behind Apollo is the will of Zeus. In plays conceived along such lines, it makes little difference how the characters feel. What matters is what they do. They are the instruments of god's justice and not much more. In the *Electra* of Euripides, however, Apollo is nowhere to be seen. Agamemnon's children act voluntarily, and their feelings before and after the scenes of butchery are dramatically contrasted. The tragic effect is deferred beyond the deed of horror and has to do with the psychic devastation of those who, in their fury, have done themselves an irreparable injury. The shift of emphasis from plot to character thus results in a marvelously effective outcome which it is impossible to resolve and which marks an extraordinary advance in the direction of realism.

The discomfort of this outcome is, of course, in some sense tempered by the appearance of the Dioscuri, so that the future of the disconsolate children is settled by divine fiat. But this is a purely mechanical expedient which is in any case not altogether convincing. What is tragic in this *Electra* is that the outcome can never be satisfactorily resolved, and with this perception Euripides immensely deepened the reach of the myth of Agamemnon.

In this play the appearance of the gods in the machine is, indeed, inexcusable; evidently Euripides found it necessary to resolve his plot at any cost. The falsity of such devices was certainly not lost on Aristotle. In the *Poetics* he noted:

> . . . the resolution of the action should arise out of the plot itself. It should not be produced mechanically as in the *Medea* or in the arrested embarcation in the *Iliad*. The god in the machine should only be used for things outside the play, for past events beyond human knowledge or events in the future which need to be foretold. For the gods are said to know everything.[48]

* * *

Tragedy indeed operates in a world in which the gods know everything. Their omniscience is shared by prophets and soothsayers, who normally live in caves, and above all by Apollo, Zeus's spokesman, who is willing, for a fee, to share his foreknowledge with those who consult his oracle. But while the oracle can indicate the future course of events, little can be done to alter that course. Destiny is relatively inflexible, and the tension between its dictates and the will of man is a prime source of tragic drama.

Man presumably has free will and is consequently responsible for his actions. But it is fate that motivates his choices. This paradox underlies much of Greek tragedy. In tragedy the divine administration is everywhere at work, but the gods seldom show themselves, and when they do, it is chiefly in the clouds, when the action is over or before it begins. The celestial powers act by indirection and generally through human agencies. The world is governed from above, but the world's work is done by men. Very often it is done badly. In the world of tragedy, accordingly, the dramatic interest centers on the human conflict, and the gods are glimpsed mainly on the margin.

Thus the logic of the type of drama with which the *Poetics* deals involves an ambiguity. The tragic hero is autonomous, but he acts under pressures over which he exercises no control. He is free, but free chiefly to suffer. At the core of Greek tragedy is the burning question which endlessly troubled those who tried to make sense of life in the course of the Christian Middle Ages, the question of free will and determination.

The problem becomes painfully evident when the tragic hero is shown to be possessed by a spirit that bewilders him. Neither Ajax nor Heracles can escape the consequences of their madness, though it is transient, nor can Phaedra or Medea. The plays that involve these characters are, of course, such that the plot is necessarily shaped by the characterization. They do not conform with the formula prescribed for effective tragedy in the *Poetics,* but they do seem to indicate the direction in which tragedy was to develop in future times. It was probably from Euripides that Seneca derived his idea of tragedy as a study of abnormal behavior, and under Senecan influence the idea gained ground in the time of Shakespeare that tragedy was the result of the soul's illness.

In both Greek and Roman psychology the perturbations of the soul are regularly ascribed to some type of daemonic possession. Ajax is possessed by Athene, Phaedra by Eros, Pentheus by Dionysus. Psychic pressures are made visible by the use of ghosts. The Greek tragedies teem with supernatural presences. In the *Antigone* Creon complains that some god possessed him. Medea is overcome by fury. But in general the Greek hero is not sick and is seldom at odds with himself: he is at odds with heaven. The conflict is hopeless, but it is robust. It takes place in the light of day, in the sun. When tragedy becomes seriously involved with character, it takes place in shadow.

In Greek tragedy the question of intention is seldom raised. Seemingly it makes no difference to Zeus that Oedipus committed his sins in an effort to avoid them or that Agamemnon was divinely constrained to incur guilt at Aulis. Unlike the Christian God, Zeus takes note of the actions of men, not of their motives. In the Greek drama the subordination of character to plot resulted in a simple and elegant outline quite different from the complex fuzziness of Elizabethan tragedy. Until the time of Euripides there is very little soul-searching in the tragedy of the Greeks. The Greek heroes move quickly; they do not have time to look into their souls. When they do, they are frightened.

The modern dramatist is inclined to see tragedy in the conflict of the individual and society, a sociological problem. The Greek poets, however, had at their disposal a broader world-view. The reality they created in the theater was a dream world with dimensions far beyond the scope of the modern playwright. Sophocles, accordingly, could account for much that is mysterious in the plays of Ibsen or Chekhov or Beckett. Oedipus suffers mightily, but there is no turmoil in his soul: he is completely at odds with the outer world, but within himself he is at peace; he has suffered, and his account is closed. It is otherwise with the the hero of modern tragedy, with Brand or Peer Gynt.

Renaissance tragedy did not imitate the Greek. The Italians and after them the Elizabethans preferred to caricature their heroes in the Roman manner. Seneca had imagined a world teeming with hysterical spirits actively engaged in manipulating the living in accordance with their own macabre interests. In the Renaissance the consequence was the series of popular plays that center on the behavior of fiend-driven villains—in England such monsters as Barabas, Edmund and Richard III; in Spain, the long procession of jealous husbands madly inflamed by a sense of outraged honor.

Until Euripides presented the *Medea* in 432, characterization in Greek tragedy steered clear of psychological analysis. In the *Philoctetes* Sophocles had developed something like a conflict in the soul of Neoptolemus. In the *Medea* Euripides struck a deeper chord. In this play, for the first time in the history of tragedy, the depiction of a psychic conflict became an essential element in the dramatic structure.

The *Medea* clearly foreshadows the *Hippolytus.* In each play the heroine's discomfort is attributed to an external agency, and in each the heroine is instrumental in bringing about the downfall of the character marked out for destruction. But while the design of these plays is the same, the characterizations are such that the plays make very different impressions.

Both plays tell stories of unrequited love, and in both the dominant motive is the revenge of Aphrodite. In the *Medea* the lovers have become enemies, and their love has turned to hate.

Something of the sort takes place also in the *Hippolytus*. Aphrodite is mischievous; in each case she inflames the heroine with love for an inappropriate person. In the *Hippolytus* the reason is announced at the outset. It is more mysterious in the *Medea*, but Jason makes his position clear. It was, he says, in order to enable him to bring home the Golden Fleece that Aphrodite caused Medea to fall in love with him. He tells Medea:

> It is my belief that it was Cypris alone that took care of me in the course of my voyage. I know that you are clever. But it was love's inescapable power that compelled you to keep me safe, not you.[49]

Consequently Jason feels no gratitude for Medea's help in getting him safely home from Colchis. Nor is he any longer mindful of Aphrodite. His adventure is over, his goal is reached, and now Medea is a nuisance to him. But in casting Medea aside for a more useful spouse, Jason is affronting Aphrodite. The towering fury that overwhelms Medea is not her own. It is the fury of the goddess that inflames her. She is possessed:

> I shudder at the thought of the harm I am doing, but stronger than my fear is my fury—fury that makes mortals do the greatest evils![50]

Medea is, of course, an exceptional woman and insists on being treated with the respect that is due her. She tells the chorus:

> Let no one think me a poor weak woman sitting at home with folded hands. I am a woman of another sort, dangerous to my enemies and a blessing to my friends. And it is women like me who are remembered.[51]

The chorus prays to Helios, Medea's ancestor, to avert the rage that possesses her:

> O light that comes from Zeus, check her and drive out
> of the house the bloody fury raised by the fiends of
> hell![52]

Euripides is scrupulous to distinguish between the character of his heroine and the power that moves her, so that the conflict in the *Medea* is elevated well above the level of a domestic quarrel. The offense against Medea is a cosmic outrage; the heavenly powers are concerned in it. Hence her revenge is inhuman, and in the end her rescue is facilitated by divine means. She escapes from Corinth in the sun's chariot. The effect is not produced, as the *Poetics* suggests, mechanically. It arises from the plot.

The portrait of Jason comes close to caricature, but the portrait of Medea is second not even to that of Oedipus as an epoch-making study of character in the drama. It is significant that it did not impress the audience favorably when it was first presented. It won third prize.

Three years later, however, the *Hippolytus* won a victory.

* * *

The *Hippolytus,* like the *Medea,* turns upon the revenge of a woman scorned, but while the *Medea* proceeds mainly on the human level, in the *Hippolytus* the gods are visible. Hippolytus is devoted to Artemis and scornful of Aphrodite. In the prologue Aphrodite tells the audience she has decided to put the fear of god into this hubristic character:

> Those who worship me in all humility, I exalt in honor.
> But those who show themselves stiff-necked in their
> pride, I destroy. In the hearts of the gods also there is
> joy when they are honored by men.[53]

Aphrodite's weapon is Eros, and since Hippolytus is armored against love's dart, she plans to strike at him through Phaedra, his father's young wife. The whole course of the forthcoming action is disclosed in the prologue. Phaedra, Aphrodite tells us, is expendable:

> Phaedra must die, but she will gain renown. Her suffer-
> ing does not weigh so heavily in the scale as to make
> me spare my enemies.[54]

Much of the play, however, is devoted to the portrayal of the expendable Phaedra. The plot, aside from the prologue and the long epilogue, is crisp and to the point. When first she appears, Phaedra is dying of love. Theseus, her husband, is presumably lost in Hades. In an effort to save her mistress, the nurse tells Hippolytus the cause of Phaedra's indisposition. The boy is revolted, and the walls resound with his anger. In the midst of the clatter, Theseus is announced. Phaedra, in terror for her reputation, writes a note accusing Hippolytus of raping her. Then she hangs herself. Theseus banishes his son with a curse. The curse works at once: Hippolytus is borne in, badly mangled, and dies at length in the presence of Artemis, who explains everything, and vows to avenge herself on Aphrodite, her rival.

Hippolytus is characterized as a remarkably stiff-necked youth, athletic, neurotic, and unduly studious. A member of an Orphic cult, he is a vegetarian and a misogynist. In choosing so inappropriate an object for Phaedra to love, Aphrodite fully demonstrates her malice as well as her sense of humor. But Phaedra understands nothing of the madness that afflicts her:

> Alas! What has happened to me? How far have I strayed
> from the path of good sense! I was mad. It was a mad-
> ness sent by some god that caused my downfall. I am
> miserable! Miserable! Nurse, cover my face. . . .[55]

What Phaedra feels is beyond her control, but what she does is done voluntarily. The false accusation is in part defensive, but in part vindictive. She is not by nature a dangerous woman like Medea, but her plight makes her deadly. As the play is designed, it is not clear whether it is Phaedra or Hippolytus or Theseus who bears the weight of the plot. But it is Phaedra who is most carefully characterized, and it is she who chiefly engages attention. Thus, in his version of the play, Racine very rightly centered his tragedy on the lovesick woman.

There is no place in Greek tragedy for the *joie d'amour* which enlivens the romances of the Renaissance and floods the Elizabethan plays with sunshine. What befalls Phaedra is not romantic love. For the purposes of Greek tragedy love is a savage appetite that ravages the lover until it is appeased—and even afterwards. The blow that is aimed at Hippolytus fells everyone within reach. Aphrodite is not a benign goddess. In his agony, Hippolytus reviles the irresponsible powers that govern the affairs of men:

Oh if men could only put a curse on the gods![56]

But the play, of course, could not end on this note. In the last scene Artemis patches up everything, and in obedience to her wish, all is forgiven. The *Hippolytus* departs very far from the idea of tragedy that Aristotle set forth in the *Poetics,* but in the year 428 it won first prize.

* * *

Ajax, presented twenty-two years before the *Hippolytus,* in 450, is among the first of the Greek tragedies to center on a portrayal of character. As Sophocles pictures him, Ajax is inordinately proud. When the armor of Achilles which he covets is awarded to Odysseus, he works himself up to such a pitch of fury that he sets out to slaughter the Argive chiefs in their sleep.

Athene prevents him from carrying out his intention. She clouds his mind so that he vents his rage on the quartermaster's herd of cattle instead. When he comes to his senses, he kills himself.

From the standpoint of the *Poetics* the plot is episodic. The play does not end with the death of Ajax. There follows a long and acrimonious conflict over the disposition of his body. But aside from the concluding agon, which principally involves his half-brother Teucer, the plot deals with the fall of a hero afflicted with hubris. Ajax has annoyed Athene by vaunting his self-sufficiency, and in the opening scene of the play the goddess takes pleasure in exhibiting her wretched victim to his rival:

Do you see, Odysseus, the greatness of a god's power? Was there any man more far-sighted than this man, or more able to act with judgment?

Odysseus answers:

None that I know of. Deeply I pity his wretchedness and his blindness, though he is my enemy; and I am thinking not only of him, but of myself. For now I see the true condition of mortal men. We are no more than dim shapes and weightless shadows.[57]

Obviously the *Ajax* was devised according to a scheme far removed from that proposed in the *Poetics.* Here the narrative is arranged so as to arouse pity by exhibiting the consequences of a tragic event as it touches the lives of those who survive it. The result is a series of vignettes held together mainly by the death of the hero. It embodies an idea of dramatic design which departs widely from the usual idea of Greek tragedy, and along with *Prometheus Bound,* it foreshadows the tragic pageant of *The Trojan Women.*

* * *

According to the third-century Roman rhetorician Aelian, *The Trojan Women* was included in the tetralogy for which Euripides was accorded the second prize in the Dionysian contest of the year 415. Its design in some ways recalls that of *Prometheus Bound.* Aside from that, it is unique among the existing tragedies. It is a tragedy of immense dramatic power that is distinguished by a plot that is wholly episodic.

The play depicts the preparations for departure after the sack of Troy. In the prologue the gods decide to destroy the victors on their way home. Meanwhile the Achaeans are busy dividing the spoils. The Trojan men have been slaughtered; the women have been herded together on the beach. In the opening episode Hecuba alone is visible, an old woman in the last stages of misery.

Like the titan of *Prometheus Bound,* Hecuba is on the stage throughout the play. Various characters come into her presence— the herald Talthybius, mad Cassandra, Andromache with Astyanax, Hector's child, Menelaus and Helen. The women are told off, one by one, into slavery, and Astyanax is destroyed. The city is set afire, and the Greeks board their ships, which Poseidon proposes to sink. The play is an interlude between two horrors, one past and one to come. There is very little action and no conflict.

The Trojan Women is a prime example of the type of drama which depends for its effect neither on plot nor on character, but chiefly on mood. It conveys no message. The massacre at Melos had taken place some months before the play was presented, and the Sicilian venture was even then in preparation, but the play says nothing explicit about war nor anything about the futility of conquest. It does say something about the human condition; but what it says is properly inarticulate, for it is at this point that the tragic transcends expression and becomes a moan or a scream. But *The Trojan Women* is neither of these. It is a solemn music, a requiem.

THOUGHT

Of the six parts of a tragedy enumerated in the *Poetics,* thought *(dianoia)* is reckoned third in the order of importance. What is meant by thought in this context is not, of course, the intellectual tendency of the play, its message, nor the opinions expressed by the author in the course of the dialogue or by way of the chorus. It is the ideas expressed by the characters in bringing about the ends they have in view, an aspect of the characterization. Since, according to Aristotle, the function of tragedy is the evocation of emotion, the author's opinions, if he has any, have neither relevance to the plot nor any place in the story. They may, of course, influence its selection or its shape, but such considerations are extraneous to its quality as drama. Aristotle expresses no interest in the intellectual content of a tragedy. His discussion of thought is limited to what the characters are made to say in the course of the action:

> . . . by thought is meant the character's capacity to say what is possible and appropriate to the occasion. It is properly considered as a branch of politics or rhetoric, for the older poets made their characters talk like politicians and the moderns like rhetoricians. Character reveals the moral status of a person, the quality that determines his choices, the things he seeks or avoids in a situation where it is necessary to choose. A speech on a purely indifferent subject does not characterize the speaker. Thought is displayed in the course of an argument or in a general expression of opinion.[58]

The relation made here between thought and character is clear. A person's character is revealed by what he says and does in the course of the action. What he says in the furtherance of his aims, however, belongs to the art of eloquence, and for instruction in devising appropriate speeches for his characters the poet is referred to Aristotle's handbook on rhetoric:

> What concerns thought may be left to the treatise on rhetoric, for the subject properly belongs to that inquiry. Under the head of thought comes whatever is said by way of proof or disproof, or in the arousing of such feelings as pity and fear or anger, or in the exaggeration or depreciation of things. It is clear also that the thoughts expressed by a character must be consistent with his actions whenever he is intended to arouse pity or fear or to exaggerate the importance or probability of something. . . .[59]

By thought, then, Aristotle means the use of language to effect a purpose; thus it serves to display the poet's linguistic ability, as well as the character of his personage. It in no way serves, however, to characterize the author, save in his ability as a craftsman. There is no discussion in the *Poetics,* nor any need for discussion, of the moral or political objectives of the poet in composing a play. In Aristotle's view the theater is not a forum for the exchange of ideas. A tragedy is neither an allegory nor an exemplum nor a vehicle for the expression of opinions. From the standpoint of the *Poetics* tragedy is designed to move, not to teach.

It is clear, of course, that in Aristotle's day there were other, and more usual views than these regarding the function of tragic poetry. In the time of Plato, certainly, poetry was generally considered a medium of instruction. Poets were teachers. The objection to poetry in the *Republic* is that poets are not good teachers. In retelling the old stories, Socrates says, the poets malign the gods and transmit dangerous ideas to the young. They needlessly awaken the passions, and in soliciting tears and laughter, they diminish the individual's capacity for self-control.[60]

In the *Frogs,* when Aeschylus asks what it is that one admires in a poet, Euripides answers, without hesitation, that it is wise counsels that will make better citizens. Indeed, Old Comedy is full of wise counsels, and Roman tragedy bristles with moral maxims. In the *Epistle to Piso* Horace laid down the principle that the aim of the tragic poet is to instruct as well as to please. This passage had wide currency all through the Renaissance and is still influential:

> The poet's aim is either to profit or to please, or to blend in one the delightful and the useful. Whatever the lesson you would convey, be brief, so that your audience may grasp quickly what is said, and may retain it accurately. . . . The elderly rail at poetry that conveys no serviceable lesson; our young patricians cannot stomach serious verses. He who mingles the useful with the pleasurable—the utile with the dulce—carries off the palm by charming, while at the same time intructing, the reader. That is the sort of book that makes money for the publisher, and is posted overseas, and assures its author of lasting fame.[61]

It is the function of the chorus, according to Horace, to edify and to instruct:

> [The chorus] must back the good and give wise counsel; it must control the passionate, and cherish those who fear to do evil; it must praise the frugal meal, and exalt justice, law, and Peace with her open gates. It should respect what is told it in confidence, and pray heaven that prosperity may visit the humble, and turn its back on the proud.[62]

In Greek tragedy, however, the chorus is seldom endowed with the capacity to fulfill such ample requirements. When it is required to utter words of wisdom, it usually confines itself to the saws of the marketplace, formal precepts, *gnome* worn smooth by time. It chides excess, counsels moderation in all things, and dwells on the folly of human pride and the dangers of hubris. It may be assumed that such sage counsel sung with flute accompaniment would be received by the Athenian audience with satisfaction but hardly with surprise. Indeed, the chorus, as an actor in the tragedy, is seldom in a position to generalize philosophically on the significance of the action. For the meaning of a tragedy—assuming it has meaning—one must look, not at what is said, but to what is done. On this basis tragedy is seldom informative. Normally it is ambiguous.

In our day such a view of drama may seem improbably limited; but the modern theater is not the theater of Dionysus. We are accustomed, in our day, to plays in which the author is much in evidence. Often he is represented by a *raisonneur*. Sophocles had no need of an actor to serve as his spokesman. He had a chorus, but the Sophoclean chorus does not speak for Sophocles. It speaks for itself and expresses sentiments appropriate to its character as an elderly gentleman or a friendly neighbor. Nor do the personages of Greek tragedy ever step out of character. In the *Ajax* Odysseus speaks in the character of the wise Odysseus. In the *Philoctetes* he is the Odysseus of many devices. But in neither play have we any reason to associate him with Sophocles. It is Odysseus that observes that we who live are no more than dim shapes and weightless shadows. We have no certainty as to what Sophocles's ideas on the subject may have been.

In the *Agamemnon* we seem to come a little closer to the author. The world that is created in the *Oresteia* is evidently ruled by laws and customs it is perilous to disregard: to defy

Themis is to invite disaster. But it is hardly sensible to conclude that this banality is what the *Oresteia* teaches. Aeschylus did what he could, it would seem, to make sense of the myths he chose to dramatize. In the *Agamemnon* the chorus is assiduous in its effort to see a pattern in the strange drama it has witnessed, but the story really defies rationalization, and the chorus concludes that the mystery is explicable only in terms of the will of God, whose motives are beyond human reason:

> Zeus, if to the unknown god that name of many is acceptable, upon him I call. I have pondered long, but I cannot find any road save that which leads to Zeus to dispel the ignorance that weighs upon my mind.[63]

In short, the chorus concludes, God only knows what this is all about. It is doubtful if many generations of careful scholarship have reached a better conclusion.

Greek tragedy takes place in an atmosphere of mystery. The world created by Aeschylus and his contemporaries is ruled by Zeus in accordance with his will and might. The myth which underlies the *Oresteia,* as well as the *Prometheus,* presupposes a cosmic tyranny from which there is in the foreseeable future no prospect of deliverance. In the *Iliad* Zeus is seen holding in hand the scales in which are weighed the lives of men, their portions of good and ill. With his other hand, presumably, he wields the lightning. There is no appeal from his decision. When he nods his head, Olympus quakes.

The *Oresteia* ends with the institution of a court of justice ruled by men. In the *Oedipus Tyrannus* the question of justice is insistent, but it is not raised. At the end of the *Trachiniae* of Sophocles the chorus sings:

> You have seen violent death and strange and terrible suffering, and there is nothing there that is not Zeus.[64]

The Greek tragedies are reassuring insofar as they affirm the existence of mind in the order of things, but they do not trace the workings of the celestial brain, and they do little to dispel the discomfort of the human condition. Zeus is inscrutable, even as the God of Job is inscrutable. He feels no need to justify his actions for the benefit of mankind. He is frightening and content to remain so. He is the eternal bogeyman who haunts our dreams, even as he haunted the dreams of those who first shuddered at the sacrifice of Iphigenia or the blinding of Oedipus.

The modern reader who tries to reconstruct for himself the sense of the implacable power that broods over the *Oedipus* plays or *The Trojan Women* may prefer to approximate its pressures more closely to the workings of Schopenhauer's *Wille* or Hegel's *Weltgeist*, the vital spirit that underlies consciousness. The god of Greek tragedy, however, has a less abstract quality. He is said to be the mind, the *nous*, that rules the world. In fact, he is depicted as a remote Homeric image, a father-figure of uncertain temper whose judgments are calculated to inspire neither love nor confidence, but rather fear and pity. In the *Oresteia* he is said to be the teacher of mankind. He is, unhappily, a singularly sadistic schoolmaster:

Zeus, who has taught man how to think, has ruled that wisdom must be learned through suffering.[65]

The world, from this standpoint, is a kind of school, and history is the record of man's rise from primitive bestiality to the peak of civility he now graces. His education, however, is likely to be thorough. If we can credit the Aeschylean chorus, Zeus will continue to beat sense into mankind as long as the world endures. The prospect is not particularly cheering:

For the heart is grieved when one remembers pain, and wisdom is not bought cheaply. From the gods in their splendor, good comes hard.[66]

Such, at least, is the opinion of the old men of Mycenae. We may be inclined to consider this the teaching of Aeschylus, but there is nothing in the *Oresteia* to justify such an inference. There is much suffering in this trilogy, but nothing to indicate that anyone is the wiser for it. Orestes, it is true, goes off whistling. But the court that was instituted to try him could not make up its mind, and his trial came to an arbitrary and somewhat bizarre conclusion. The play, obviously, was not designed as an exemplum.

The *Poetics* rejects the idea that the function of tragedy is to teach. But Horace, among others, accepted that idea without question, and it was most acceptable to the Renaissance. In the sixteenth century, Giraldi voiced a widespread opinion:

The function of our poets, then, with respect to influencing morality, is to praise virtuous actions and to blame vices, and by means of the terrible and the fearful to make them odious to the reader.[67]

On this point, however, there was no consensus. Castelvetro wrote:

Those who hold that poetry was invented chiefly for the benefit it confers, or in order at the same time to benefit and to delight, should beware of opposing the authority of Aristotle who here and elsewhere does not appear to assign any end to tragedy other than pleasure. If indeed he admits of some profit, he grants it only incidentally, as in the purgation of terror and compassion by means of tragedy.[68]

It was, of course, important in those years to defend poetry against the strictures of the church by emphasizing its moral utility, and the attempt to reconcile the views of Plato, Aristotle and Horace gave rise to much controversy with regard to the function of tragedy. Mazzoni, Sidney, Tasso, Guarini, and Scaliger all took sides in a cacophany of critical opinion which, in the circumstances, admitted of no resolution at that time—nor, it may be added, at any other.

INVENTION

T HE MYTHS THAT provided the materials of Greek tragedy
were sanctified by tradition, but they were not permitted
to crystallize into the rigidity of monuments. The poets of the
fifth century treated the old stories with reverence, but they did
not scruple to reshape them imaginatively when it suited their
purpose. The myths were not absolutely inflexible. They accepted manipulation, and were thus constantly available for
poetic purposes, especially in the theater.

Poetry, according to the *Poetics,* deals with things not in
their actuality, but in their essential aspect. What was enacted
in the theater, consequently, was an ideal history designed to
arouse an effective emotional experience. Practically, this was
achieved, as we have seen, with the help of music and dance,
through a sequence of acted episodes, linked in the order of
cause and consequence, proceeding logically to a predetermined conclusion. The function of the dramatist was, accordingly, to transform fact into fiction, and thus to create what
Cézanne called, in another context, a reality parallel to nature.

This type of *mimesis bion* necessarily entailed invention,
but the poet's scope as mythmaker was limited, for the fifth-
century audience evidently preferred fact to fiction and re-

warded plays based on stories authenticated by tradition rather than those of uncertain authenticity. In the *Poetics,* such preferences, as we have seen, were justified in terms of credibility:

> . . . what convinces is the possible. Now, while we are not sure of the possibility of what has not yet happened, what has already happened is clearly possible, since it could not have happened were it not possible.[1]

In time, however, the dramatic poet was accorded wider scope. Aristotle cites the *Antheus* of Agathon with approval as an example of a plot that was wholly invented:

> A poet must not limit himself strictly to the traditional myths on which the best tragedies are based. It would be ridiculous to do so since even the best known stories are known only to a few, though they give pleasure to all.[2]

It is clear, indeed, that the fifth-century poets did not assume that the myths they dramatized were known to all. In the surviving tragedies whatever is necessary for the understanding of the narrative is regularly set forth in the prologue or recited in the parodos, and as the play progresses, the audience is constantly kept informed of the state of affairs. In the theater, the Greek poets strove above all for clarity, and made little use of suspense or ambiguity to stimulate the audience. In what is termed in the *Poetics* a "complex tragedy which is all peripety and discovery," the unexpected comes as a surprise more often to the characters of the drama than to the spectator. If the audience is surprised, it is rather by the reaction of a personage to the event that affects him than by the event itself. In the *Hippolytus,* for example, the entire plot is revealed by Aphrodite in the prologue, and is then acted in detail precisely as it was planned.

The range of subject matter in the great age of Greek tragedy was, without doubt, far wider than that exhibited in the
existing canon. In the *Poetics* many tragedies are mentioned of
which no trace remains. Of the plays that have been preserved,
those that deal with domestic horrors appear to have been
especially effective. In discussing the nature of the tragic plot,
Aristotle observes:

> At first poets dramatized whatever tragic tales they hap-
> pened to find, but now the best tragedies are based on
> the legends of a few houses, such as those of Alcmaeon,
> Oedipus, Meleager, Thyestes, Telephus and others to
> whom it came to do or to suffer terrible things. In
> theory, the best tragedy will have a plot of this descrip-
> tion. . . . The proof of this is that in the contests, and
> on the stage, tragedies of this sort are the most effec-
> tive, provided they are skilfully handled.[3]

Apart from Telephus, the son of Heracles, the characters
named in this passage are all constrained to injure someone to
whom they are bound by natural ties. In Aristotle's opinion the
tragic effect is best evoked by the representation of a deed that
arouses sympathy for its agent as well as for its victim:

> Let us see, then, what kind of events are terrible and
> what sort are pitiable. . . . The parties must either be
> friends or enemies, or else people indifferent to one
> another. Now, when an enemy acts against an enemy,
> there is nothing to arouse pity, either in the deed or in
> its anticipation, except in the actual suffering it entails,
> and the same is true when the parties are indifferent to
> one another. But when the tragic deed involves those
> who have love for one another, as when brother kills
> brother, or a son his father, or when a mother kills her
> son, or a son his mother—these are the situations a

poet should look for. The traditional stories, accordingly, must be kept as they are, for example, the murder of Clytemnestra by Orestes, and Eriphyle by Alcmaeon. At the same time, even in these cases, there is something left for the poet to do. It is for him to devise the proper way of treating them, and to use skilfully what is handed down to him.[4]

The tragic in Greek tragedy was, of course, not limited to themes of this sort, but the ties of the family and the clan were of paramount importance in classic times, and the deeds of Agamemnon, Orestes and Alcmaeon must have aroused a powerful emotional response in the fifth-century theater. In our day we tend to think of the tragic element in these ancient horrors in terms of the inner conflict of the reluctant hero and the social pressures that determine his behavior. These are considerations that do not seem to have been of interest in the drama much before the time of Shakespeare. In his *Critique* of *Le Cid* Corneille cites the *Poetics* with reference to the tragic plight of lovers torn between the demands of desire and duty. Subsequently, the conflict of love and honor becomes indispensable to the tragic characters of the age. It was obviously not this sort of love that Aristotle had in mind in recommending plots of this shape to the poets of his time, but from the standpoint of dramatic construction, the precept in the *Poetics* was certainly influential in determining the course of tragic drama in the age of the baroque.

The formal similarity of the existing Greek tragedies tempts one to underestimate the range of the Greek poet's inventiveness. We cannot judge the quality of the predecessors of Aeschylus, but from the available evidence it is arguable that Aeschlyus virtually invented tragedy in the form that we know. It is clear, also, that Sophocles made many innovations, and the originality of Euripides was great enough to give offense to those who disliked change. While the contemporaries of Euripides seldom ventured far beyond the outlines of the traditional myths, Euripides gave a new shape to much of the thematic material he took in hand. After *Iphigenia in Tauris, Alcestis,* and *Helen,* the way was open and inviting for Agathon and his contemporaries to invent plays that had no basis in the Homeric tradition. Since what was actually accomplished in this regard has not been preserved, it is impossible to judge the result.

According to the *Poetics,* what principally concerns the poet after the choice of his subject is the arrangement of the plot; it is in this respect that he is expected to show originality. Judging from the plays, however, it is evident that the Greek poets displayed originality more readily in characterization than in plot structure. It is useful in this connection to recall the successive portrayals of Electra and Orestes in the course of the century with relation to the plot of their tragedy.

In the *Choephoroi* Aeschylus depicts Electra and Orestes as the wretched offspring of a disastrous marriage. Electra is first seen among the house servants, her only friends. She is indignant and resentful, but hardly impassioned in her prayer for revenge. Orestes comes to the rescue under orders from Apollo, whom he fears, and is beset by the Furies as soon as his work is done. The characterizations are perfunctory. The characters are instrumental. The emphasis is on the plot.

Sophocles entitled his play *Electra,* and centered the action upon Electra. In his version of the myth, all the accents are heightened, and the motivation is magnified far beyond the reach of the *Choephoroi.* Electra is announced by a shriek of anguish offstage. When she appears, she delivers an impassioned speech that fully expresses her grief, hatred, and fury. She has been brutally treated in her father's house, and her complaints have made her presence unbearable to the point that she is in danger, her sister Chrysothemis tells her, of being consigned to a cave where her screams will not be heard. It is at this juncture that Orestes reveals himself. He is attended by Pylades and his pedagogue. It is the pedagogue who plans everything, but from the outset Orestes and Electra eagerly anticipate the murders Orestes is about to commit. In this tragedy, it is clear, Sophocles undertook to overshadow the work of Aeschylus by elevating the emotional tone of the action to a level close to frenzy.

But while he emphasizes to the full the sorrows of Electra and the magnitude of her fury, Sophocles also manages to elicit some measure of sympathy for Clytemnestra, who has to put up with a daughter who is driving her mad. The difference between this play and its predecessor in the *Oresteia* is thus principally a matter of the characterization. The plot is the same, but the plays are entirely dissimilar in their dramatic effect: the murders in the *Choephoroi* are on the whole rather businesslike and elicit something like satisfaction, whereas in Sophocles's *Electra* the action proceeds on a plane that approximates hysteria.

Euripides's *Electra* takes place in a pastoral setting with green trees and flowing brooks. Electra is introduced dressed as a peasant, carrying a waterpot on her shaven head. It develops that Clytemnestra has rid herself of her daughter by marrying her to a local farmer, whose offspring will have neither a claim to the throne nor any cause for revenge. The girl is unhappy, but she is calm and resigned. She has no need to scream. Her situation speaks for itself.

The peasant whom Euripides invented in his version of the story is very courteously portrayed so as to contrast the nobility of simple people with the shabby pompousness of the gilded rich. It is he who speaks the prologue. An old retainer takes the place of Sophocles's pedagogue. A useful character, he arranges the recognitions and the strategic details of the revenge.

Sophocles uses the stratagem invented by Aeschylus to introduce Orestes into Clytemnestra's palace. Euripides uses a very different device. He has Electra lure Clytemnestra to her hut by asking her to make the sacrifices for the supposed birth of a grandchild. The result, again, is to shift a measure of sympathy to Clytemnestra and thus to enhance the pathos of her death. Aegisthus, who is contemptible in the *Choephoroi*, is portrayed in a more humane light, and when Orestes appears in the course of the action with the body of the slain Aegisthus, Electra is unwilling to have the corpse desecrated. The result of these changes is a tone of pathos that singularly pervades the horror of the situation. Electra is indeed implacable in her revenge, but after the deed is done the children are wretched and remorseful. They do not triumph. It is left to the Dioscuri to resolve their future, and when their fate is decided, they part in sorrow, never to meet again.

The contrast between this version of the Electra story and the preceding versions tells us something of the role of the poet as mythmaker. Aeschylus was obviously not much interested in Electra: in the *Choephoroi* we lose sight of her in the middle of the play. The story is the story of Orestes. In Sophocles's version Electra is central. She is a dangerous and not entirely sympathetic character, like Ajax: the whole play is about her, and her effect on the people around her. In the hands of Euripides, Electra becomes pathetic, perhaps sentimental, but she gives one something to think about.

Aeschylus's trilogy won a victory in 458 and was, by all accounts, a great popular success. Sophocles's *Electra* cannot be accurately dated, but it was certainly accounted a masterpiece. Euripides's *Electra* does not appear to have aroused enthusiasm when it was first produced. It was not among the plays with which the younger Euripides won a victory after his father's death, and it was the last of Euripides's plays to be studied in the Renaissance. It was omitted in the edition of

1503 and was first printed in 1545. Evidently both ages preferred a more vivid Electra.

But in our time Euripides's *Electra* seems particularly appealing, and the play has something that to us seems precious. It has charm, a quality that is largely lacking in Western drama before the time of Lyly and is hardly evident in tragedy before Shakespeare showed what could be done in the tragic genre by way of enchantment. It is perhaps along these lines that Euripides's inventive genius was most fruitful, and it is perhaps in this respect that he most clearly foreshadows the drama of the succeeding ages.

At any rate, the pathos of his portrayal could not have been wholly lost on his contemporaries. When Lysander the Spartan was contemplating the destruction of Athens, he happened to hear a minstrel singing the *"Agamemnos o kore"* from the first chorus of Euripides's *Electra.* [5] The Spartan general, we are told, burst into tears. The Acropolis was saved.

It is necessary to believe such stories.

CATHARSIS

I T IS, OF COURSE, possible that in predicating his idea of tragedy on its therapeutic value, Aristotle was concerned to justify the Dionysia as an official institution supported by public funds. Plato had excluded poetry from his republic on the ground of its educational shortcomings. For Aristotle, as we have seen, the social benefit of poetry had not much to do with education.

Aristotle's assumption that the function of tragedy, its final cause, was the release of emotional tensions, was no doubt related to medical theories widely current in his time. The Hippocratic school considered disease to be caused by an imbalance of the bodily humors, the result of which was a harmful excess of one of the vital fluids. Under favorable conditions the healing power inherent in the human body might be expected in such a case to expel the morbid matter by the process of coction. The physician's aim, accordingly, was to attend the patient's fever to its crisis in order to facilitate the expulsion of the toxic substance, after which the *vis mediatrix naturae* would reestablish the physical harmony upon which health depends.

The tragic effect described in the *Poetics* apparently involved an analogous treatment of the emotions. Through the influence of the dramatic action on the imagination of the spectator the morbid spirits that normally beset the heart would be inflamed to the point of crisis, and then dispelled in an emotional outburst which might elicit tears. The spectator would then leave the theater purged of his fears and anxieties, in a state of mental health.

It is amusing to consider that a scientist of Aristotle's stature meant to justify the tragic contests as a means of administering a psychic purgative to the Athenian citizenry in the spring of the year. But it is possible that in attributing a therapeutic aim to the drama Aristotle saw more deeply into the purposes of the theater than those who justified it as a means of entertaining the public or appeasing the gods.

We have no idea of how things were managed in the theater of Dionysus in the time of Sophocles. One may imagine a rocky hillside crowded with people, resonant with the shouts of actors, the shrill of flutes and the stamping feet of the dancers. Doubtless the audience was intent when the action concentrated its attention. At such times the throng of closely packed spectators, warmed by the sun, the play and one another, must have come as close to madness as do the spectators at a sporting event in a modern stadium. Guy de Maupassant aptly describes the effect of a sermon in a provincial church in a corner of northern France in the nineteenth century:

> Men and women, old men and lads in new blouses were soon sobbing. Something superhuman seemed to be hovering over their heads—a spirit, the powerful breath of an invisible and all-powerful being. . . . Suddenly a kind of madness seemed to pervade the church, the sound of a crowd in a state of frenzy, a tempest of sobs and stifled cries. . . .[1]

Experiences of this intensity are relatively rare in the modern theater. It is to the musical orgies of our day that we look for such examples of collective hysteria. The little we know of the ancient theater, however, indicates that the tragic effect alluded to in the *Poetics* resulted in something more impressive than a round of polite applause.

In our theater the audience seems most self-contained when it is most deeply stirred, and it is only at stated intervals that the auditorium calls attention to itself. We know it was not always so in the modern playhouse. It was not until the end of the nineteenth century that the English theater developed its stately manners along with its carpets and a scale of prices designed to exclude the obstreperous. In the ancient theater, under conditions not unlike those of a modern soccer match, the tragic contests might be expected to generate a certain degree of heat. Since Greek tragedy was designed to arouse powerful emotions, Plato's objection to tragedy as a dangerous business suggests that the theater of his time was far from placid. In Plato's *Ion* the rhetor describes the dramatic fervor of his performance:

> When I am describing something pitiful, my eyes fill with tears. When it is something terrible or strange, my hair stands on end, and my heart throbs. . . . And whenever I look down from the platform at the audience I see them weeping, with a wild look in their eyes, lost in wonder at the words they are hearing.[2]

The implication here is that the storyteller at the height of his performance is no longer himself but is possessed by the spirit that animates him. In this condition he is physically radiant, and the god in him is readily transmitted to those who are privileged to participate in his act. The audience and the performer are then beside themselves, in a state of ecstasy.

In the light of modern clinical experience, Aristotle's idea of the function of tragedy seems cogent. The singular predicament of Oedipus in ancient Thebes can have little relation to anything in the conscious experience of a modern spectator, and it can hardly be expected to arouse anxiety in a modern mind. The same might have been said, doubtless, in the time of Sophocles. The enormous power of the play of Oedipus indicates, therefore, that the play speaks not to the intellectual faculty of the beholder, but to the infantile mind that underlies it. Evidently in the suburbs of our consciousness we dwell at no great distance from ancient Thebes, and in that vicinity Oedipus may well be a near neighbor. Since the play of Oedipus is still capable of stirring up pity and terror, its energy evidently has its source not so much in the myth of Oedipus as in the fantasy that gave shape to the myth. In that fantasy, it has often been shown, we have all had at some time a share.

Aristotle's hypothesis with regard to the purgative effect of tragedy is thus entirely in accord with modern psychological theory, provided it is assumed that the plane on which drama operates lies some distance below the level of the rational faculty. Diderot long ago observed that the domestic difficulties of the ancient heroes have not much to do with the troubles of contemporary life. But the tragic myths do not seem to tarnish, and the tensions that produced them have not relaxed. Whether they are costumed in chiton or jeans, the characters of Greek tragedy are equally effective as a source of tragic poetry, for, as Aristotle noted, the roots of tragedy are familial, domestic:

> Whenever the tragic deed is done within the family, as when brother kills brother, or a son kills his father, or a mother her son, or a son his mother, or contemplates doing so, these are the deeds that the poet should look for.[3]

While the idea that tragedy is an emotional purgative may find acceptance in psychiatric circles, the suggestion that the tragic plays were systematically administered as a laxative each spring might well provoke a smile. It is perhaps more reasonable to relate the pleasure, as well as the efficacy, of the tragic contests to the rites of Dionysus of which they certainly formed a part.

With the exception of the *Bacchae*, none of the surviving tragedies has anything to do with the myth of Dionysus, and in comedy only the *Frogs* concerns the god of the theater. The Bacchic rites, so far as is known, did not at first involve the drama. Impressive evidence has been adduced to show that in early times sacrificial practices in honor of Dionysus and Demeter assured the renewal of the seasonal cycle. The dithyrambic and dramatic contests seem to have been late additions to the ceremonies that honored the god. The dithyrambs were doubtless intended to flatter Dionysus, but it is difficult to see in what way the performance of tragedies might be thought to further the germination of the barley or the sweetness of the grape.

Dionysus was a foreign god. In the *Bacchae* he is said to have hailed from Lydia. Perhaps he came from Thrace. In any case, he was evidently adopted by the Olympians at a time when it seemed wise to assimilate his cult to the official religion of Greece. Zeus then became his father and Theban Semele, the daughter of Cadmus, his mother, and he rapidly acquired a host of divine relatives. A vase painting now in Leningrad shows Apollo extending a welcoming hand to Dionysus in the sacred precincts of Delphi.

Dionysus did not take up his abode in the sky. He was of the earth, a chthonic deity. Unlike the Olympians, he knew suffering. He was periodically sacrificed and resurrected. And he knew joy. His presence, when he chose to manifest himself, was intoxicating, delectable, and dangerous. Normally it was transmitted from the earth through the fermented juice of the vine.

What is known of the mystery religions suggests that the rites of Dionysus, like those of Osiris, Mithras and others, included a periodic sharing of the god by his worshippers, a eucharist. In the more primitive stages of the cult, apparently, his vicar, the sacrificial victim, was human. At some point in the course of the ritual, the priest who embodied Dionysus was torn apart and eaten by his worshippers. In this manner the participants were filled with god and became godlike. In later times, it appears, the god's divinity was transmitted by the rending, the sparagmos, of his vicar, the sacred bull or goat which embodied his spirit. At a still later stage of his cult these bloody sacraments must have seemed unduly savage. In the *Bacchae* the description of the rending of Pentheus was certainly calculated to inspire the audience with horror, and while in this play the joyful side of Dionysus is also developed, the angry god is shown to be both terrible and merciless, the god of tragedy.[4]

Tragedy means "goat song." The etymology is clear, but the connotation is puzzling. It has been conjectured that in its early stages tragedy was performed by men clad in goat skins; however, there is little evidence to support this assumption. In the *Bacchae* the Bacchantes wear the skins of fawns. Dionysus was, among other things, a bull. In the dithyrambic contests a bull was the victor's prize.

The prize awarded in the tragedic contests was, it is said, a goat. Dionysus Eleutherius, the god of tragedy, was called melainaigis, the Black Goat. It was his image that was carried from his shrine in Eleutherae to his altar in the theater, and it was his priest that presided over the performances. It is reasonable to suppose, in the absence of evidence, that the god in the theater was somehow identified with the goat awarded to the victorious contestant, perhaps for sacrifice. If one wishes to think of tragedy as a goat song, there is no lack of goats to support the idea.

Unlike such exercises as the footrace and the wrestling match, drama affords no certain ground on which to base a judgment of excellence; the verdict is necessarily subjective. In the Dionysian contests the judgment would be based, no doubt, on the judges's taste and experience, as well as on the volume of applause that the plays elicited. Since Greek tragedy served a religious purpose, one might expect a display of skill in the theater to be offered in tribute to Dionysus in the same way that displays of strength in the Pythian games were offered as a tribute to Zeus. But it is difficult to understand in what way a display of tragic suffering might be pleasing to Dionysus. On the other hand, it is understandable that tragedy was intended not to amuse the god, but to invite him to share himself with his worshippers.

Following the suggestion in the *Poetics,* it may be supposed that in the theater of Dionysus the aim of the performance would be to produce in the audience the state of ecstasy which Lavoisier, in his report on Mesmer, called *l'unité d'ivresse,* a mass hysteria, induced by hypnotic suggestion, in which the individual loses sight of himself and merges his life with the collective life, the universal consciousness. If this happened in the Greek theater, it might well be said that the audience experienced Dionysus: it shared the god spiritually just as his body and his blood had once been shared physically. Tragedy, then, was not a sacrificial offering; it was a eucharist. It is not likely that this is what Aristotle understood as the tragic effect, but it is possible.

The suggestion is tempting because this magic can still be managed in the theater. When the play works, as every actor knows, something uncanny takes place in the playhouse, and the normal mummery of the stage is miraculously transformed into a reality beyond ordinary experience. The play is blessed, and those who are there are touched by grace, for they have experienced god. Such moments, unhappily, are rare in the modern theater, but when they happen (it is very noticeable), the participants are no longer strangers. They are bound by an ineffable bond and are reluctant to part, and in the street they obstruct the sidewalk.

One may suppose that when this happened—if it happened—in the theater of Dionysus, the judges had no difficulty in reaching a verdict.

The religious aspect of the theater has been written about so often in recent years, and so fervently, that one is moved to brush the idea aside as a commercial promotion. But in fact, it is in anticipation of a transcendental experience that we endure the annoyances of the playhouse, and the intensity of our disillusionment when we leave the theater unfulfilled is commensurate with our hope when we enter it. The service of Dionysus has at all times been arduous, and it is rarely rewarding. But those whom Dionysus has touched, his thiasos, frequent his precincts as fervently as ever. To the churchgoer the theater may seem a strange place to look for God. But many have sought him there.

The song of the goat, whatever its origin, was by the time of Aeschylus very far from the scream with which the slaughtered animal yielded up its spirit. In tragedy the threnos might begin with an inarticulate cry. Often it does. But the threnody is invariably a work of art, the lyrical consummation of the tragic action that produces it. At this point the tragic hero is usually depicted at the height of his agony, but while the powers of destruction can deface him, they have not the power to stifle him. In his pain he sings, and the chorus sings with him.

We may reasonably conclude, in line with the principle of the *Poetics,* that the aim of tragedy is the stirring up of disquieting emotions—not, however, in order that they may be dispelled, but that they may be sublimated. It is indeed remarkable that this can be made to happen. The capacity to transform pain into pleasure is, without doubt, the basis of art in general, its aesthetic principle, but tragedy seems to have been devised expressly to demonstrate this ability. It is an invention that fills one with awe at the ingenuity of the human spirit, an achievement which in its sheer utility dwarfs the conception of the wheel or the electron microscope:

> There are many wonders, and none more wonderful than man, he that sails the storm-swept seas, cutting a path through the waves. And earth, the eldest of the gods, the ageless and unwearied, he wears down, turning the furrow with the offspring of horses as the ploughs go up and down from year to year. . . .
>
> And speech, and thought that speeds like the wind, and the lore that can found cities, all this he has taught himself, and how to bear the frost and take shelter from the rain. For all things he finds a way. He is never at a loss with the ills that come, save only with death, which no man can escape. . . .[5]

It is in such passages that we sense the mood of tragedy.

NOTES

Greek Tragedy (Pages 8–13)

1. Giovanbattista Giraldi Cinthio, *Discorsi intorno al comporre de i romanzi, delle comedie e delle tragedie* (1543), Venice, 1554, p. 220.

2. A. Diamantopoulos, *Journal of Hellenistic Studies,* 67, part 2, pp. 200 ff.

Greek Theater (Pages 14–20)

1. A. F. Haigh, *The Attic Theatre,* 3rd ed., Oxford, 1907, p. 35.

2. A. W. Pickard-Cambridge, *The Theatre of Dionysus in Athens,* Oxford, 1946, p. 174.

3. Aristophanes, *Frogs,* 1009.

4. See T. B. L. Webster, *Greek Theatre Production,* London, 1956, pp. 174 ff.

5. A. W. Gomme, *The Population of Athens in the Fifth and Fourth Centuries B.C.,* Oxford, 1933; George Thomson, *Aeschylus, Oresteia,* Cambridge, 1938, 2, p. 357.

6. A. W. Pickard-Cambridge, *Dramatic Festivals of Athens,* Oxford, 1955, p. 175; Webster, *Greek Theatre Production,* pp. 35, 199 ff.

The Actors and the Chorus (Pages 21–27)

1. A. E. Haigh, *The Attic Theatre*, 3rd ed. Oxford, 1907, p. 278.

2. Aristotle, *Poetics*, ch. XVIII. 1456 a 25. References are to page numbers in Bekker's edition of the works of Aristotle. These are marginal in the Loeb edition, Harvard University Press, 1953.

Play Construction (Pages 28–48)

1. Aeschylus, *Agamemnon*, 466.

2. Ibid., 922.

3. Ibid., 944.

4. Ibid., 1500.

5. Aeschylus, *Choephoroi*, 301.

6. Ibid., 322.

7. Ibid., 510.

8. Ibid., 1074.

9. Aeschylus, *Eumenides*, 639.

10. Sophocles, *Antigone*, 594.

11. Ibid., 666.

12. Ibid., 677.

13. Ibid., 781.

14. Ibid., 1271.

15. Ibid., 1347.

16. Ibid., 620.

The *Poetics* (Pages 49–105)

1. Plato, *Republic*, 603 D. See Gilbert Murray's preface to Ingram Bywater, *Aristotle on the Art of Poetry*, Oxford, 1920.

2. Aristotle, *Poetics,* ch. IV. 1449 b 9.

3. Ibid., ch. IV. 1449 a 9. Cf. John Harington, *Poetry into Drama,* University of California Press, 1986.

4. Aristotle, *Poetics,* ch. VI. 1449 b 20.

5. Ibid., ch. VI. 1450 b 16.

6. Ibid., ch. XXVI. 1462 a 14.

7. Ibid., ch. XIV. 1453 b 1.

8. Ibid., ch. VI. 1449 b 31.

9. Ibid., ch. VI. 1450 a 19.

10. Ibid., ch. IX. 1451 b 35; 1452 a 1.

11. Ibid., ch. IX. 1451 a 36.

12. Ibid., ch.XIV. 1453 b 1 et seq. Antonin Artaud, *Le Théâtre et son double.* In *Oeuvres complètes,* 9 vols. (Paris), 1956–71, vol. 4, p. 161.

13. Aristotle, *Rhetoric,* II, 8.

14. Ibid., II, 5.

15. Aristotle, *Poetics,* ch. VII. 1450 b 34.

16. Ibid., ch. V. 1449 b 7.

17. Horace, *Ars poetica,* 23.

18. Ibid., 143 ff. See E. H. Blakeney, *Horace and the Art of Poetry,* London, 1923, and see text in Augusto Rostagni, *Arte poetica di Orazio,* Torino, 1930.

19. Lodovico Castelvetro, *Poetica d'Aristotele vulgarizzata e sposta,* (1570), Basel, 1576, ch. 6, p. 109.

20. Ibid., ch. 24, p. 535; cf. ch. 3, p. 57.

21. Pierre Corneille, *Discours des trois unités* (1660). In *Théâtre complet.* 1 Paris (Pléiade), 1957, vol. 1, p. 129.

22. Jean Racine, "Préface de Bérenice," (1671). In *Oeuvres complètes (Grands Écrivains de la France),* vol. 2.

23. Corneille, *Discours,* p. 132.

24. Aristotle, *Poetics,* ch. VI. 1450 b 21.

25. Ibid., ch. VIII. 1451 a 16.

26. See Torquato Tasso, *Discorsi,* iw *Opere,* Milano, 1826, book 3, pp. 27, 31–32; Lope de Vega, *Arte nuevo de hacer comedias* (1609), translated in Barrett Clark, *European Theories of the Drama,* New York, 1929, p. 89.

27. Aristotle, *Poetics,* ch. XVIII. 1455 b 24.

28. Aristophanes, *Lysistrata,* 566.

29. Aelius Donatus, *De Comoedia et tragoedia,* edited by P. Wessner, in Gronovius, *Thesaurus Graecarum Antiquitatum.,* Venetia, 1735, vol. 8, translated in Clark, *European Theories of the Drama,* p. 43.

30. Aristotle, *Poetics,* ch. XII. 1452 b 14.

31. Ibid., ch. X. 1452 a 11.

32. Ibid., ch. XI. 1452 a 22.

33. Ibid., ch. XIII. 1453 a 12.

34. Ibid., ch. XIII. 1453 a 30.

35. Ibid., ch. XI. 1452 a 29.

36. Ibid., ch. XIII. 1453 a 7.

37. Sophocles, *Oedipus Tyrannus,* 977.

38. Ibid., 897.

39. Plato, *Republic,* II, 380 D.

40. Aeschylus, *Agamemnon,* 772.

41. Ibid., 750.

42. Sophocles, *Oedipus Tyrannus,* 874.

43. Herodotus, *History,* III, ch. 125.

44. Aeschylus, *Agamemnon,* 1005.

45. Herodotus, *History,* III, ch. 10.

46. Aristotle, *Poetics*, ch. XV, 1454 a 15.

47. Giraldi, *Discorsi* (1549), Venice, 1554, ch. 63.

48. Aristotle, *Poetics*, ch. XV 1454 b 2.

49. Euripides, *Medea*, 527.

50. Ibid., 1078.

51. Ibid., 807.

52. Ibid., 1259.

53. Euripides, *Hippolytus*, 6.

54. Ibid., 44

55. Ibid., 239.

56. Ibid., 1417

57. Sophocles, *Ajax*, 118.

58. Aristotle, *Poetics*, ch. VI. 1450 b 4.

59. Ibid., ch. XIX, 1456 a 33.

60. Plato, *Republic* II, 337 B and 337 F. Cf. X, 603 C.

61. Horace, *Ars poetica*, 333.

62. Ibid., 189.

63. Aeschylus, *Agamemnon*, 160.

64. Sophocles, *Trachiniae*, 1274.

65. Aeschylus, *Agamemnon*, 176.

66. Ibid., 179.

67. Giraldi, *Discorsi*, (1554), Venice, 1549, p. 59.

68. Castelvetro, *Poetica*, 1571, ch. 23, p. 505.

Invention (Pages 106–113)

1. Aristotle, *Poetics*, ch. IX, 51 a 36.
2. Ibid., ch. IX, 51 b 19.
3. Ibid., ch. XIII, 53 a 12.
4. Ibid., ch. XIV, 53 b 1.
5. Euripides, *Electra*, 166.

Catharsis (Pages 114–122)

1. Guy de Maupassant, *Madame Tellier's Excursion* (1881).
2. Plato, *Ion*, 535 A.
3. Aristotle, *Poetics*, ch. XIV, 1452 b 3.
4. Herodotus, *History*, III. 48. Cf. L. R. Farnell, *Cults of the Greek States*, Oxford, 1896–1909, Vol. 5, pp. 65, 301, 303; M. P. Nilsson, *A History of Greek Religion*, Oxford, 1949, p. 205; Erwin Rohde, *Psyche*, London, 1925, p. 286; Margarete Bieber, *The History of the Greek and Roman Theater*, Princeton, 1939, p. 22. For further enlightenment on this point, see A. W. Pickard-Cambridge, *Dithyramb, Tragedy and Comedy*, Oxford, 1962; J. E. Harrison, *Themis*, 2nd ed., Cambridge, 1927; George Thomson, *Aeschylus and Athens*, London, 1941, pp. 247 ff.; H. D. F. Kitto, *The Greeks*, London, 1951; U. von Wilamovitz-Moellendorf, *Die Glaube der Hellenen*, Berlin, 1932, vol. 2, pp. 60 ff.; B. Hunningher, *The Origin of the Theater*, Amsterdam, 1955, pp. 32 ff.; A. Lesky, *A History of Greek Literature*, New York, 1966, *passim*; *Greek Tragedy*, New York, 1965; G. F. Else, *Aristotle's Poetics*, Harvard, 1957; John Jones, *On Aristotle and Greek Tragedy*, Oxford, 1962.
5. Sophocles, *Antigone*, 332.

INDEX